AMAZING GRACE

Anita Bryant

G.K.HALL&CO.

 Boston, Massachusetts

1973

Library of Congress Cataloging in Publication Data

Bryant, Anita.
  Amazing grace.

  Large print ed.
  1. Bryant, Anita.   I. Title.
[ML420.B84A28   1973]   784'.092'4   [B]   73–9985
ISBN 0–8161–6136–4

Scripture references in this volume are from the *King James Version of the Bible.*

Published in Large Print by arrangement with Fleming H. Revell Company

Set in Linotron 18 pt Times Roman

To Charlotte and Dan Topping and their family whose experience of the AMAZING GRACE of God contributed so much to this book

Contents

AMAZING GRACE

1   God Takes Over

You may be surprised to learn you're actually reading, at this moment, the last page of this book. I've come back to the beginning to write it. As Bob Green, my husband, surely will say, "Anita insists on always having the last word!"

It amazes and awes me to see how much of what follows has happened in just these past six weeks at Villa Verde, "House of the Greens," at Miami Beach, Florida.

We'd started out to share with you in these pages some of the high spots in our adventures as parents, Christians, and show business people. Then God took over. And how! He has turned these past few weeks at our house into some of the most glorious days of our lives.

Tumultuous, joyful, yet painful days—and it all began on a very ordinary afternoon in our kitchen where Bob and I discussed (or to be honest—argued!) about this book.

"Why in the world did you let me get myself into this, Bob?" I asked him. "You know I don't have it made as a Christian. Who am I to be writing books? I sure don't want to project myself as a Christian who thinks she knows all the answers when really. . . ."

"Something's about to burn," Bob said calmly, lifting a lid from one of the pots. "Nothing important, though. Just carrots."

"Oh-h-h-h! Don't dare try to change the subject, Robert Green," I sputtered. (I always call him *Robert* when I get mad at him.) When I start getting cold feet about something I take it out on my husband, who also happens to be my business manager. But Bob's pretty unflappable.

"Anita, do you know how many calories there are in carrots?" He whipped out a little book and consulted it. "No carrots for me. Just roast lamb and spinach, thanks."

I just gave him a cold stare. As someone who thinks of himself as a new Christian (Bob was saved the night before our wedding, nearly eleven years ago), my husband well remembers his decision for Christ, his

2

commitment, baptism, and coming into the fellowship of the church.

He still feels new in the faith, eager, interested, with everything ahead of him. By contrast, he sees me as quite old in the Christian life, since I was saved as a child of eight. Does he imagine, therefore, that it's all very automatic and easy for me? Suddenly I felt overwhelmed.

Why can't Bob understand? Doesn't he know I've been in a strange sort of turmoil lately, besieged at times with deep doubts about myself? Can't he see that this is no time for easy answers?

"Anita, of course you don't have all the answers," he said, guessing my thoughts. "Who does? Just go ahead and tell it like it *really* is. Doubts and disagreements as well as victories. Unanswered prayers, too, like when the whole family was praying for me to stick to my diet. . . ."

"You should have let God help you, instead of diet pills!" I put in.

". . . and let this be your witness to the fact that God really can transform us ordinary people when we accept Jesus Christ as our Lord and Saviour," he finished.

Witness! Bob's forever pushing me to witness. I want to, but he simply doesn't have any idea of just how hard it is—how inadequate and unworthy I know I am, how . . . oh, I'll have to pray about it.

"Pray about it, Anita," Bob suggested.

That man! Sometimes he reads my mind. But little did either of us dream that God would begin that very night to set our prayers in motion.

Dinner is on the table. We're all seated, hands folded, heads bowed for the grace. Mealtimes with four young children sometimes can turn into a real three-ring circus. I take advantage of this quiet moment to steal a quick look at the blond heads around our table.

Bobby, age seven, sits at Bob's right and Gloria Lynn, six, at her father's left. At the other end of the table I sit on the firing line between the two high chairs, with two-year-old Billy to my right, his twin sister, Barbara, to my left.

It's Bobby's turn to say grace. "God is great, God is good. Let us thank Him for our food. In Jesus' name, Amen," he prayed.

"A-a-a-a-MEN!" the twins boom out loudly, in sudden and perfect unison. Everybody starts to laugh.

"Sh-h-h-h," I warn, frowning at the older children. "Let's don't encourage them to clown about that." The giggles stop.

Funny how at certain moments you realize exactly how rich you are—how you wouldn't change one thing about your life. Now that everybody's eating and chatting so nicely I can look at them and really see how lucky I am. A handsome, wonderful husband who really loves his family. These adorable children. . . .

"Oops!" You have to move fast. "No, Billy and Barbara, no bread and butter until you eat some vegetables and meat." I grab the bread, the twins' favorite part of the meal, and move it out of reach. This seems a signal for bedlam to begin.

"Ugh. I can't eat my meat. There's fat on it," Bobby says in a voice of despair.

"Son, you know better than that," Bob reproves him. "You know how to cut your meat. Use your knife, and. . . ."

"Quick, Mommy!" Gloria interjects. "Barbara's eating Bobby's bread while he

5

complains about his meat!'' Indeed, Barbara is doing just that. I snatch the bread away.

''All gone!'' Billy roars triumphantly. His plate is miraculously clean. No wonder. While I took Bobby's bread away from Barbara, Billy hid his meat and vegetables beneath his plate—a trick he thinks nobody can see. When I pick up his plate and begin to put the food back on it, he looks quite dismayed. Loud giggles rise around the table.

''Bobby and Gloria, please don't laugh at Billy,'' I warn. ''That's naughty,'' I tell our small son, sternly.

''That's *naughty!''* comes an echo from his twin. Her severe tone of voice sounds identical to mine. No use to tell them not to laugh. Everyone's laughing, even Bob.

When I turn to reprimand Barbara my heart almost catches in my throat. She's a bewitching baby with her bright yellow hair and blue eyes, deep dimples and wide smile. She's a Swedish doll—a Christmas tree angel.

But my angel hasn't eaten a bite. When I start to feed her bits of meat, some carrots and spinach, she balks.

''Bread and butter, *please.* Bread and butter, *please,''* she insists, pressing her lips

6

together and firmly refusing her carrots.

"No bread and butter until you eat some dinner!"

"But I *said* the magic word! I *said please!*"

"Don't laugh at Barbara," I begin again. But it's no use. They're all laughing now, and I'm laughing too. You can't keep a straight face forever.

So it goes, on a typically hectic day in an average American household. And then it's bedtime for the little people.

First, the twins. Bob and I take turns cuddling each baby, telling each how much he is loved. Then, kneeling between the cribs, Bob and I fold our hands and bow our heads. The twins copy us. They look so cute I only half-close my eyes so I can watch them pray. I know Bob does the same thing.

"Now I lay me down to. . . ." Bob and I begin together.

"*Sleep!*" said Barbara.

"I pray the Lord my soul. . . ."

"*Keep!*" Billy busts in triumphantly.

They always take turns chiming in. They're so sweet and serious, but also they're comical. It's terribly hard not to smile.

And then we're tucking them in, giving

each little face one last kiss. Already Billy's brown eyes are closing. Barbara's shine blue as ever, but she has begun to suck sleepily on her pacifier.

Now Bobby and Gloria creep in to kiss their brother and sister good-night, and give a loving pat to the drowsy heads.

These really are God's babies, I think, as the four of us tiptoe out of the nursery. They really seem to understand about Him, so naturally and joyously.

Gloria Lynn tugs on my arm, then reaches up to whisper in my ear. "Mommy, Mary's crying."

Mary Hendrick, one of our household helpers, is weeping as she talks on the telephone. Obviously she's receiving bad news.

"I'll come right back and see about Mary, honey. Prayers first, though."

At our prayer altar, Bob reads from God's Word. Then each of us prays aloud, in his own words, for people and situations close to our hearts. Gloria immediately prays for Mary.

How close we're becoming as a family, since Bob installed this altar. And soon the twins will be old enough to join us. . . .

Every one of us loves this simple ritual. As we walk toward our children's bedrooms, they continue to share with us.

"I told Horatio about that pin they gave me at Sunday school. The one shaped like a fishhook," Bobby said. "I explained it has nothing to do with fishing. It means you're supposed to tell other people about Jesus. Jesus wants us to be fishermen for Him."

Horatio and Bobby, "best friends," have talked about Jesus a lot since they attended vacation Bible school together last summer.

Gloria, sober-faced, has less happy news. She and Wendy, her especially beloved friend, had a bad spat today. "Why don't you ask Jesus to help you be a better friend to Wendy?" Bob suggests.

"Okay, Daddy." Her troubled face lights up in a smile.

Suddenly I'm really tired. I've promised the kids a bedtime story, but first I must see about Mary. The news she received is so bad, her grief is so terrible, I hardly know what to say. I sink to my knees before her and put my arms around her.

"Mary, shall we pray about it?"

But what comfort can I really give her? I

keep trying to find the right words. Suddenly I'm out-and-out witnessing to Mary, telling her Christ can meet all her needs. I'm amazed to hear my own spontaneous testimony.

At the same time, I feel cold fear in my stomach. My thoughts are in a turmoil. Much as we all care for Mary, I'm afraid I'll fail her now. I simply don't know how to approach her.

"I can't pray now," she sobbed.

I hesitated, dreading to ask the next question yet knowing I must: "Mary, do you know Jesus Christ as your personal Saviour?"

Even as my lips speak these words, my mind forms an urgent prayer. *Lord, I'm not ready for this. I can talk about You in a stadium filled with people, at Billy Graham crusades, on television and at church. I can even write a book about the miracles You performed in my life. But this, dear Lord, I cannot do of myself. Jesus, take away my fears and replace them with Your love. Please help me witness to Mary!*

It was a desperate prayer. Afterwards, however, I feel nothing.

"Are you saved, Mary?" I ask again.

She stared at me in surprise. "You know

I'm religious, Mrs. Green. I pray all the time. If I didn't pray I'd go out of my mind.''

If ever I've wanted to flee from anything, now is the moment. How can I witness to this devout Roman Catholic woman without seeming to intrude on her faith—or to criticize it?

Suddenly I feel an overpowering burden for Mary. A kind of gentle boldness—a sureness I've never felt before in my life—sweeps over me.

''The Bible says in Acts 4:12, concerning Jesus, *Neither is there salvation in any other: for there is none other name under heaven given among men, whereby we must be saved.* You should pray in the name of Jesus,'' I told her.

''I believe in Jesus.''

''Yes, but even though you were baptized and confirmed. . . .''

''All this was done. I've been a Christian all my life.''

''Yes,'' I said. ''But your parents made that decision for you, didn't they? Have you, from your own sound mind and body, ever made that commitment personally? In God's Word He says, *Ye must be born again.* There has to

11

be a time and a place—whether it be now, in a closet, in a church, or wherever—that you realize you are lost and need Christ. You must choose Him.

"You chose everything else, Mary—your husband, your profession, your way of life. You also must choose Christ. Being raised in a Christian home doesn't make you a Christian."

Suddenly I can see it makes sense to Mary. Now is the moment of truth. I am terribly afraid. Mary is listening and thinking. Her crying has ceased. It's time to ask the question.

"Mary, will you pray that prayer with me?"

I look straight into her eyes, silently pleading with her. There's a terrible silence in the room. The moment stretches out.

"No. I don't want to."

Help me, Lord, I prayed. "Mary, I'm not talking about being a Baptist or a Catholic. I'm talking about being sure you have Christ in your heart."

"But I can't. I don't know how," Mary says in a small, sad voice.

"God tells us how in Matthew 18:3

. . . . *Except ye be converted, and become as little children, ye shall not enter the kingdom of heaven,"* I tell her. "Just open up your heart. Your wanting Jesus to come into your life is all that's necessary." I literally hold my breath as I wait for her answer. Surprising to see how much it hurts, how my own heart feels literally torn, as though it might burst with pain.

"Yes." Her answer comes so softly.

I take Mary's hand and we pray together for about three or four minutes. We just lay it on the line, as simply as possible. "God, we're praying for Mary's soul now. We ask you to come into her heart so she'll have the assurance that she knows You. Give her the peace of mind and soul to comfort her in all her needs. . . ."

At last I ask Mary to say with me, "Jesus come into my heart." At that moment she was really eager. She didn't hesitate.

Thank You, Lord. Oh, thank You, thank You!

The thing that has swollen inside me seems to burst as Mary says those words, and tears rain down. Something inside me literally breaks, and continues to break, and is washed away by my tears as I see Mary come to Christ.

When we finished praying Mary says, "Thank you. I feel better now." She promises to begin reading her New Testament every day. As I help Mary to bed, we share a strange new peace.

How long have we prayed together? I have no idea. I only know I feel so empty—so exhausted—it's an effort to climb the stairs.

The children are asleep. Bob is in bed also, and our room is dark.

"Anita, I'm very proud of you." Bob's voice sounds gentle.

"Why?" I ask, astonished.

"Because you witnessed to Mary. You set a good Christian example for our children."

"Oh Bob, I promised to read to them. . . ."

"Never mind—they understood. I asked if they knew what you were doing and they said, 'Mommy's being a fisherman.' They were praying for you, Anita."

I cannot describe my feelings of that moment. A sudden shyness. A deep sense of awe. But most of all, the clear realization that my Christian husband and our children

—loving and understanding me—supported Mary and me with their prayers. And now Mary belongs to Christ!

Yet I, Anita Bryant, nearly . . . oh, almost . . . didn't witness to Mary. *Lord, even as I prayed so desperately that You would remove my fear, these little children prayed also! Your grace is more than sufficient in this household tonight!*

Suddenly I'm flooded with joy and gratitude. I know quite simply that God has changed my life in some profound way I can't yet define, even as He changed Mary's. There in the dark, I try to express these things to Bob. I can sense his understanding.

Yet that night neither of us dreamed God had grasped some of the loose threads of our lives and begun to weave them together. Nor could we imagine how, in the next amazing weeks, He'd begin to resolve some unspoken dissatisfactions, ongoing dilemmas, and unanswered questions in our lives.

Certainly I couldn't know that these as yet undreamed-of events—together with some earlier adventures—would be included in this book!

2 Super Joy

Talk about pressures!

Bob and I had just been to New York to tape the Kraft Music Hall TV Special, "On Stage, Miss America."

Then the Christmas season arrived, with the kids' school activities, extra cooking, and all the rest of it. We still had the telecast of the Orange Bowl Parade ahead of us, with a TV taping of the Junior Parade to do. And this was the year we had booked to sing at the telecast of the Orange Bowl football game, and —biggest challenge of all—the telecast of the Super Bowl game.

Happy? I sure should have been. Any of these bookings is great. Add them all together, however, and the total spells P–A–N–I–C. I began to get very uptight.

Then came the morning everything inside me broke loose.

"Don't ever book me again!" I told Bob.

17

"I never want to do *anything* again. I can't take it. I'm getting too old for this kind of thing. It's too much!"

Bob didn't say a word. Instead of criticizing me or badgering me, he simply went to his office. Just before I left for the telecast (I was to commentate the Orange Bowl Parade with Joe Garagiola) Bob slipped something into my hand. When I looked to see what it was, I felt decidedly irritated to see a small prayer encased in plastic. It read:

> God grant me the serenity to accept the things I cannot change, courage to change things I can, and wisdom to know the difference.
>
> REINHOLD NIEBUHR

"Ah, baloney," I told myself at first.

However, as I went through a long day of rehearsals and taping, I began to realize how that prayer hits home. I remember how hard I worked to get to this point in my career. Now God is bringing me good work, opportunities I should be profoundly grateful for—and I want to chuck it all!

My attitude seemed especially selfish when

18

I thought about Bob. He has given enormous amounts of his time, talents, and energies to my career. Actually, he works three times as many hours as I do, and much of what he does is the sort of important but tedious detail work that would drive me crazy. I'd never be where I am today without Bob's hard work, but he's too often the unsung member of the team—strictly a silent partner.

Anita Bryant, do you really have the idea you're in this thing all by yourself? I asked myself, feeling deeply ashamed.

Still, the pressures.

I couldn't seem to do anything about these tensions that accelerate steadily before every performance—especially those where we play to thousands of people. This is nothing new, of course. Inside I'm still the eight-year-old girl back in Oklahoma, getting carsick on the way to her first television audition.

Tensions are part of the game, I told myself. The emotional buildup, the worry, the pressures that carry you up and up into a sort of emotional high that lets you give everything to a performance—to sing your heart out for them—will always be my way of life.

But this year was different. "Success" in

the form of one major booking after another meant just one thing. I could not wear myself into an emotional frazzle, could not afford the tension headaches and all the rest of it. Unless I changed my emotional makeup, I just couldn't last.

When you think about it, *my* part in the booking was relatively small. All I had to do was sing! The Missouri band, however, rehearsed "Battle Hymn" for three months before the game. Meanwhile, Bob, the network people, and the Orange Bowl and Super Bowl committees worked their heads off to make stadium history. They placed microphones before every important band instrument, and speakers every few feet throughout the huge stadium, so guests could hear.

On those two occasions, people in the stadium could hear as well as if they were at a recording session. It was marvelous, phenomenal sound—and it stopped ninety thousand bowl-goers in their tracks.

As all these advance preparations got underway, I became more and more nervous. Ernie Seiler and Dan McNamara of the Orange Bowl committee and members of NBC-TV staff conferred with Bob more and more often.

Audience reaction at the Orange Bowl, where those ninety thousand people remained awesomely silent as I sang our national anthem, should have calmed my fears about the Super Bowl.

Yes—fears. I felt scared to death—and didn't know why. The voice was fine. Goodness knows I've sung those numbers thousands of times. And Bob, Chuck Bird, our conductor-arranger, and everybody else connected with the music, the sound, the network and the stadium were in terrific accord.

But something was wrong with me —something I couldn't even define. It was worse than fear or worry or depression—it was the heavy feeling of a burden too big to carry, yet too urgent to put down.

As time went by I became increasingly uptight about the Super Bowl. I began to get the feeling that every celebrity in America would be right there for that game. Besides the thousands of people who would pack the stadium, millions more across the nation would watch our performance on television.

This would be the largest audience of my

career. I felt more and more shaken as I realized that. Above all, this would be no time for little Anita to get carsick!

Sunday morning dawned bright and beautiful on the day of the Super Bowl. Bob and I were due at the stadium soon after noon. I wouldn't be able to go to church that day, but I decided to get up early and take the children to Sunday school.

Silly? Maybe so. I could have forfeited Sunday school and perhaps been a little more relaxed for my performance.

"Somehow something tells me to make that little effort," I told Bob. I knew, somehow, that God would honor such efforts, and would supply what I needed within myself that afternoon at the Super Bowl. If I didn't begin my day at the Lord's house, I reasoned, the Holy Spirit surely couldn't be close within me as I performed.

It was hard to keep my mind on our lesson that morning, though I needed Sunday school that day as I never had before. At last I blurted out to my classmates (who are a close-knit group of young wives and mothers in my age bracket) that I felt a terrific burden about the Super Bowl.

"Please pray for me," I begged.

"We'll all pray for you exactly at 3:15, when you go out to sing. Don't worry, Anita," Kathy Miller, my friend and Sunday school teacher said.

Brother Bill Chapman, our minister at Northwest Baptist Church, and his wife, Peggy, gave me the same reassurance. "We'll ask the entire congregation to support you with prayers," they said.

At the stadium, as I stepped on a lift which carried me to the fifteen-foot high float from which I was to sing, I suddenly became aware of how many separate things might go wrong—and ruin my performance. For example, there were twelve guys out there handling twelve mikes. Split-second timing was involved, and any number of technical things might bomb. The audio setup was intensely sophisticated.

As the lift ascended, I began to pray for the performance. I thought about our church and the many, many loving individuals praying for me at that very moment.

The instant I stepped onto the frighteningly high platform from which I'd sing, a thrilling sense of freedom suddenly possessed me.

Beyond me sat a crowd of many, many thousands of people. Above the vast stadium bowl a brilliant blue sky burned like a flame. My heart leaped within me and I felt intense, inexpressible joy—a joy I'd never, never before in my professional life experienced.

God's Holy Spirit!

How lovingly He had appeared to comfort and empower me. Without Him I would have felt indescribably alone—a mere dot stationed high above a wide sea of people.

But no. Instead, I felt exalted, enthroned within a circle of love so endless, so widespread, it could not be comprehended. Miraculously the frightened, tense, insecure Anita had vanished. Filled with the presence of the Holy Spirit, Bob Green's timid wife had become calm and utterly serene—certain that God willed me to be there at that moment for His purpose.

If only Bob could share this with me, I remember thinking.

He did, in a way. Bob Green, after all, knows every note and every nuance of all the songs I perform. He knows my fears, too, as well as my very deepest hopes and aspirations. But above all, Bob understands exactly what singing means to me—especially when I'm singing to the glory of God.

That day God prepared me—my friends' prayers prepared me—to sing the monumental "Battle Hymn of the Republic" as I've never before sung it in my life.

As my voice lifted the first stirring words, it seemed as though everything I was—voice, body, and spirit—literally floated on a cloud. And at that moment I knew something I'd never before known so truly in my entire performing life.

"This is how God means it to be!" something inside me fairly shouted. "Pure joy! Joy too thrilling, too intense, to be shared in any other way at all."

This is why God created song.

I've never before put these feelings into words for Bob. But there's no need to. He knows. He really knows.

3 On Stage

When I have to do something hard—and when I get sick at my stomach, fearing I don't have the courage and strength—I just say Bob's prayer over and over to myself.

Surprised? Well, now I'm leveling with you.

It's terribly hard to explain what performing does to me. In some ways it seems like the very breath of life. In others, it almost seems to consume me.

I use myself up when I perform. If I don't go all the way, give everything, I feel like I'm not doing my best.

"Sometimes it seems so painful for me. Like too much," I complained to Bob. "I don't understand myself any more."

What can Bob say? He knows I could no more not sing than I could not breathe. When I perform—I'm on. I love it. My ego is totally fulfilled. I'm reaching out to people and they're responding—and nothing else in this world matches that exultation.

Afterwards, however, comes exhaustion and (to be honest!) very often a strange, empty depression. It's almost like a miniature death—a giving and giving, until everything is used up and I feel nearly annihilated.

But the Super Bowl performance felt totally different from all that. I knew I was being used by the Lord as never before. Instead of being depleted, the experience actually buoyed me up and left me with energy to spare.

Everything that happened afterwards reinforced my knowledge that God had been present with power that day. Ernie Seiler and Dan McNamara said they'd never before experienced anything like my performance. Extravagant compliments flowed in for hours. As you can imagine, that thrilled me. However, in a real way, other people's reactions didn't too much matter. I still felt too amazed and awed by what had happened to me. I knew the credit belonged to God.

Late that night the phone rang. It was Lou Kusserow who produced the NBC show. "Anita, I just had to tell you I've never seen anything like this in my entire career," he told me. ''Never before on nationwide television—especially at a sports event—have I heard anything so meaningful and with so much soul in it!''

He continued to praise me to the point that I could hardly believe my ears. Producers don't get excited that way. That's when I really knew the Holy Spirit had gotten through. You'd never expect a network professional to react to your performance in any personal way. Therefore, his words meant more to me than all those of my relatives and friends. He confirmed my belief that I'd been used by the Lord that day.

Our act, in essence, has grown out of our home and represents our life. Bob and I travel to cities and towns all over America playing to business and international civic club conventions, state fairs, giving concerts, making television appearances, or I appear as a spokeswoman for such American businesses as the Florida Citrus Growers.

We play to the world's best audiences. By that I mean they usually include typical American families, so we present only the sort of material that portrays what we stand for as a family. The act offers pop tunes, a segment of country and Western and then, after a quick change of costume and a complete change in mood, we go into our serious finale. This segment includes such numbers as ''The Power and the Glory,'' ''God Bless America,'' and ''Battle Hymn of the Republic.''

We always close with ''Battle Hymn.''

We've never had any trouble with audiences accepting these patriotic and sacred numbers. People have come to expect this sort of act from me—not only accept it, in fact, but want it.

Increasingly, these songs have become part of my witness. When I sing ''God Bless America,'' for example, I'm aware that Americans yearn for exactly that. I play to a real cross section of America. People's reactions convince me that they feel a tremendous need for God to bless America again.

As for ''Battle Hymn,'' I do it more and more as a hymn, not a battle song. I emphasize more the coming of Christ. Our battle today is that of living for Christ.

There came a night, however, when for the first time I feared to sing the serious part of my act. We played a Miami Beach convention which was running late. Our show didn't start until nearly ten o'clock.

The audience was quite weary. They'd had a full day of meetings, speeches and a banquet, and by now some were getting restless. Two other acts preceded ours: a dance team first, then a well-known comedian.

The comic act didn't get anywhere. Desperate at the audience's lack of response, the comedian finally resorted to using blue material—very distasteful stuff.

Meanwhile, we were waiting in the wings. Bob looked at Chuck, Chuck looked at Bob, and then they both looked at me. "They're eating that stuff up. Want to chuck the last segment of the show?" they asked.

"Oh, ye of little faith!" I replied, real sharp and nasty. Though I sounded disgusted, however, I felt upset too. I could see what was happening to the audience—and I was scared. My hands were perspiring. I wondered if they'd boo me off the stage if we tried to do the patriotic and religious part of the act.

None of us really knew what to do. When we conferred Bob strongly suggested that I do no more than "Battle Hymn" for the closing portion—and maybe I'd better cut even that.

"Naturally it's your decision," Bob said. "However, that's what I think would be best with this audience in this situation."

"Let's play it by ear," I said at last. "I'll signal Chuck when I go offstage to change to the long gown. I'll decide at that moment whether I plan to return at all, whether we'll do just 'Battle Hymn' or, if a miracle happens, we'll do the whole bit."

The decision must be a last-minute one, obviously, and it must be mine. As I surveyed that restless and rather raucous audience, I doubted that they'd accept any Sunday school stuff. I prayed hard before I went on.

Lord, just lead me. The situation is Yours. I can't do anything about it. Somehow, please give me a sign.

But the sign I prayed for really didn't appear. We managed to warm up the audience a little, true, but as the act progressed I felt more and more shook up. I really couldn't tell what they wanted. Meanwhile, as Bob watched the audience from the wings, Chuck sent questions to me with his eyes.

What to do?

Suddenly I decided to plunge in and give them the whole thing. I'd bluff my way through. Right or wrong, the courage to continue appeared from somewhere within me. Too, I think there was a certain element of adventure there. No audience ever had turned me down. Would this become the first time?

I had to find out. So, to Bob and Chuck's dismay, no doubt—I swept back in there and, filled with fear and defiance, did "Power and Glory," Then we went into "God Bless America," and something happened.

They were crying. They stood up on their feet like something I've never seen before or since, and filled the room with whooping and hollering and bravos.

Then *I* stopped the act. I broke down like a baby. I couldn't stop crying. I guess I'd given everything, and something had to snap. And then I did something strange I'd never before done with an audience.

"I'm going to level with you," I told them. "I'm not crying because of your standing ovation. I'm crying because I nearly cut out the last segment of this show because I didn't think you'd like it."

That brought down the house. And when we

went into our closing number, "Battle Hymn of the Republic," that audience and I were as one body. Their ovation after the hymn actually was a near-sacred experience.

I feel funny telling about that show because I broke an unwritten rule: You *never* level with your audience. It certainly astonished them. They'd been going lower as the evening wore on, until my act asked them to come up again. They reacted as though they wanted to thank me for this.

Though that performance seemed devastating to me, it proved that even in an ungodly situation—where you think the tide can't be turned—God still can use you.

There's always the danger of forgetting that. For example, I had begun to get impatient with the pop numbers I do. I had begun to consider them a waste of time—the portion of my show that doesn't witness.

Then came the night God showed me this isn't so. Again, we were performing at a convention at one of the leading hotels here on the beach. Dick Shack, my agent of the Agency for the Performing Arts, approached me.

"One of the ladies on the entertainment

committee would like her daughter to meet you after the show," he said. "There seems to be a bad situation between them, however. Maybe a case of teen-age rebellion or something."

That night we got tremendous reaction to the last segment of our show, and people poured backstage to meet me. I noticed a little girl, maybe fourteen years old, standing apart from the others. Her long blonde hair framed a cute little face, and she seemed very shy. She waited until everybody else left the area and just stood there, waiting. This was the girl Dick wanted me to talk to, and her name was Becky. When I walked over and introduced myself she started to cry.

"You seem able to help everyone else. Can you help someone who's completely lost?" she sobbed.

"Becky, I can't help you. I can do nothing. Jesus Christ is the One who can help you," I told her, surprised at my own frank testimony. As I put my arm around the child, I felt a sinking in my heart. Despite my inadequacy, I knew God sent this child to me for my witness.

"Let's go into the dressing room," I

suggested, Now a sizeable crowd of newcomers had gathered to speak to me. "Keep them occupied. I need a few minutes for this little girl," I whispered to Bob.

"I have nobody to turn to," Becky sobbed when we were alone. She poured out a sad tale of rejection, self-hatred, despair, and the feeling that nobody in this world loved her.

"God loves you," I assured her. "In the Bible, His holy Word, He tells us that over and over." I read John 3:16 to her, and the beautiful verse 8 from the first chapter of Romans: *But God commendeth his love toward us, in that, while we were yet sinners, Christ died for us.*

I knew nothing about her parents or her life, but I did know God loves her. I felt led to tell her all parents aren't good parents, but even if this were true in her case, God still could bring her through her difficulties.

"Wouldn't you like to be right with our Lord, Becky?" I asked her

"I don't know how!"

"Let's just pray together," I said, sounding much more calm than I felt. We got down on our knees. Outside, Bob was knocking on the door. He had no idea what was happening, and people were getting impatient

Very simply, I helped Becky pray that Jesus would come into her heart. This is a strange time, a strange place, for a young girl's conversion! I thought. Then I kissed her, quickly scribbled her address—and opened the door to our fans.

Later, Brother Bill Chapman, our pastor, helped find a pastor in Becky's town who visited her and invited her to his church. I telephoned Becky and advised her to get herself a *Scofield Reference Version of the King James Bible*, and to find a good, fundamental, Bible-believing church home where she'd find the kind of Christian friends who'd strengthen her faith.

Bob and I talked more than once about that strange evening. "It really scares me to witness person-to-person that way," I told him. "Especially right after a show, when I feel completely empty anyhow!"

"What better time for God to take over?" he pointed out.

I always shall remember Becky who blessed me in a way she didn't know. Only through unexpectedly leading a child to the Lord via a contemporary situation could I realize that *anything* we do can be necessary and perhaps even essential to God's purposes. We really screen our pop music. Love ballads, yes. But some of the cheap, suggestive lyrics that push the pleasures of drugs, alcohol, and free love, definitely no! I'd become somewhat unenthusiastic about pop songs because it's getting harder and harder to find really sweet ones.

But pop music related to that little girl. If I had been speaking in a church or some similar place, I never would have met Becky. God taught me once again—through her—that He can use anything we'll dedicate to Him.

That night He took the pop music I looked down on, and used it to His glory!

4   Saved by Grace

"Why do the people go down to the front, Mommy?" Gloria whispered.

Though Bobby and Gloria had been coming for some time to "big church" with Bob and me, her question caught me off guard. She wasn't yet six. I wondered what kind of answer she'd best understand.

"They want to ask Jesus to come into their heart. They want to become saved and have all their sins forgiven!" I told her.

"I love Jesus. I want to go down too," she said immediately.

I felt a twinge of dismay. "No, Gloria, you must wait until you're old enough to understand what you're doing," I told her. I could see my answer didn't convince her in the least. "Are you old enough to get up and walk up to the altar by yourself, then?" I asked.

"No, Mommy. But you can go with me."

I didn't, of course. Later Bob and I talked it

over, and decided she couldn't possibly be old enough actually to understand what was happening.

"She's much too young," Bob said. "When her desire grows so strong she's willing to go down in front of all those people by herself, that's different. In two or three years, or whenever she's old enough, we'll know it."

I agreed with Bob. Together we explained to Gloria as best we could that when she got to be a big girl she'd want to make that commitment. Then she'd be ready to walk up the aisle on her own.

However, the same scene began to happen more and more often: the tug on my skirt, then the whisper that she wanted to go down front. "Are you willing to go by yourself?" I always asked.

"No, I'm scared. I want you to go with me, Mommy," she answered, hanging her head.

This went on for months. Sometimes we'd have serious discussions about it after we got home. I realized she had become aware that she needed Jesus in her heart, that she sinned like all the rest of us. This had begun to get to her.

To make things worse, she began to come to our bed at night crying, saying she was scared she was going to die and go to hell. We couldn't imagine where she got such an idea, but nevertheless it was firmly fixed in her head. Each time, we'd sit down and talk to her.

"No, Gloria, God would not make you accountable at this age," Bob and I told her. "You would not go to hell."

Now Bob's parents, Farmor and Farfar Green, began telling us we'd been too fanatical about our children's religious training. Anybody could see it was having an adverse effect on Gloria, after all. They weren't the only ones who thought that, I'm sure. Bob and I had to think very seriously about what was happening.

Farmor and Farfar (*Farmor* means "grandmother" and *Farfar* means "grandfather" in Swedish, their native language) love our children dearly. Always they come in and substitute for us when Bob and I travel. We wouldn't dream of leaving our children with just anyone, so they literally have made our way of life possible.

Farmor and Farfar, however, don't totally

share our Christian convictions, though they approve of our Christian household. Now they began to wonder if we were forcing religion on our children to the extent that it could do some damage. Farmor got quite upset.

"Don't put fear in their hearts," she pleaded.

"This fear has nothing to do with us, Farmor," we told her. "We don't know where it comes from. God will have to help us work this problem out."

Needless to say, I felt quite concerned. These episodes happened several times, with Gloria crying and upset. I was afraid *only* her fear of going to hell was motivating her toward going forward at church, and of course we didn't want this.

"The time will come when you know you want to be saved, and you'll want to make that commitment public," we told Gloria. "Until that time—and it may be a long time away—you are protected. You are watched over by the Lord. You still sin, but God doesn't hold you completely accountable until you're old enough to fully understand."

Despite all we could say, Bob and I saw there still was turmoil in Gloria's mind. We

42

agreed to stand firm, however. We didn't want Gloria to feel that unless she made a public commitment right away she'd be in danger of eternal punishment. We continued to stress that we come to God out of love, not just fear.

The whole thing began to get very frustrating for all of us. But as Gloria continued to tug on my skirt, I'd shake my head firmly. I knew she still did not fully understand, so we continued to have long discussions. These talks made me know she loved Jesus, that Jesus was in her heart, and I felt she was moving toward the young but very real sort of commitment to Christ which I had made at age eight.

When I thought of the longing, the strong urge to follow Jesus that carried me forward then, Gloria's tender years and her timidity simply didn't seem to compare at all.

Gloria became six in May. Big brother Bobby, our son, would celebrate his seventh birthday in September. So when it came time for our church to hold vacation Bible school that summer, suddenly it seemed I must participate.

"I feel strongly led to help," I told Bob. "I know it won't be easy, but it seems to me this is a vital summer in the kids' lives. They're both seeking God so.''

It meant we had to cancel some bookings and really juggle our work schedule around, but Bob didn't object. Our children's Christian education means much to him. Also, he'd often heard me tell how much my little sister Sandra and I had loved vacation Bible school when we were children.

What fun! It really brought back memories of my own childhood, too. The children had prayed about who they'd take with them. Gloria invited her little friend Wendy, and another favorite, Laura Morgan. Bobby took Horatio. We also invited the five children of Dan and Charlotte Topping, but they didn't want to go. I drove us to church, taught a class, then took everybody home. In the car, the children entered into fascinating discussions about God and Jesus.

''I never dreamed they could understand so much,'' I told Bob. ''It's worth the trouble of going every day—just to hear these conversations.''

''We want them to have a concern for their friends, too,'' Bob pointed out. ''They're old enough to begin to share Jesus.'' So we felt very glad we'd taken the trouble—lost money too, really, through canceling bookings—to participate. Obviously this was a perfect summer to involve myself with Bible school.

Neither Bob nor I, what's more, possibly could foresee how the Vacation Bible School at Northwest Baptist Church in North Miami could prepare Bobby and Gloria for their salvation. Certainly that was the last thought in my mind one hot night in late July, as I prepared to sleep in the room just off the nursery. The twins' nurse had the night off, so I slept near them. Little Bobby wanted to sleep with me.

Sometimes I let Gloria or Bobby help with the twins which makes them feel big and special. This was Bobby's night. Unfortunately, he felt very talkative that night. I felt tired out and just wanted to go to sleep.

Then Bobby began to talk about knowing and loving God. He brought up the subject; I wasn't in any frame of mind to discuss it, but I said, "Bobby, do you know Jesus Christ as your Saviour? Have you asked Jesus to come into your heart?"

"Oh, yes!" he said, and my own heart almost stopped.

"When did that happen?" I asked, amazed.

"During Bible school."

"Why Bobby! Why didn't you tell me?"

"Oh, well," he shrugged, a little embarrassed. "It happened in class. I didn't want to make a big deal out of it. They just suggested that we ask Jesus to come into our hearts, so I did."

I was really shocked. Bobby never had mentioned such a thing, even during those discussions in the car. I wondered if he'd just gone along with the rest of the class, or if it had been a real decision for him.

"Do you remember the exact day you asked Jesus to come into your heart?" I asked cautiously.

"No."

"When you grow up, wouldn't you like to be able to look back and remember the very day you made that commitment?"

"Sure," he said. So we got out of bed, went down on our knees, and I led my son in prayer. Then he prayed his own prayer, saying, "Jesus, please come into my heart so I can really know You and love everybody."

At that moment I felt terribly thrilled and excited. I phoned our bedroom and woke Bob up.

"What do you want?" he asked, real grumpy. Of course I wanted him to share this significant moment, so he came right down. All three of us prayed together.

Afterwards Bobby felt somewhat excited and wiggly. "Mommy, does this mean I have to go down in front of all those people in church?" he asked.

"No, son, that's a decision you have to make," I told him. "Mommy and Daddy can't tell you where and when. You must decide. When you love Jesus and ask Him to come into your heart you want to do what God tells you to do in your life. The Bible, God's inspired Word, tells us we must confess our sins before men and make our commitment to Him public. One way to do that is to go before the church and say we love Jesus and want to be baptized and become part of His church. This helps us grow as Christians.

"Bobby, in Matthew 10:32 Jesus says, *Whosoever therefore shall confess me before men, him will I confess also before my Father which is in heaven.* Public confession is like taking a stand for the Lord. You wouldn't want always to keep this a secret among just you and Daddy and Mommy.''

We could see he understood. ''I'm not going to do it yet,'' he said. ''I'll think about it and when the right times comes, I'll go down.''

''That's fine, Bobby,'' his father assured him.

When Bob and I later discussed the surprising events of that evening, we felt happy about them. We believed our son had made a sincere commitment. We didn't want to push him any further, however. We could tell he still felt a little shy about the public part.

''Let's just cool it,'' Bob suggested. I agreed.

Bobby had been saved on a Wednesday night. As the week wore on, he told us several times he didn't think he'd go forward on Sunday. We could tell he was thinking about it—maybe dreading it. We didn't want that.

''That's right, Bobby,'' his father said. ''You might want to wait a year, or until you grow up, or maybe even never. You might not want to join our church. Later you may decide you want to join another denomination. This is for you to decide.''

We saw it was working on him. I didn't dare say a word lest I influence him one way or another. That week in Sunday school, I shared my dilemma with our class. "I don't want to push him or influence him. On the other hand, if the Holy Spirit is working in him, I want Bobby to have the courage he needs," I explained.

We all prayed for Bobby that morning. As he walked into church with me later I smiled at him, sure he would feel no apprehension.

Brother Bill Chapman, our pastor, was on vacation that day so Brother Claude Wilson, our associate pastor, preached. The sermon held real power. As the message gripped me, I remember wondering once if Bobby heard it that way too—and if he'd step out this morning to commit his life to Christ.

When we sang the invitation hymn, though, Bobby didn't move. It was Gloria who tugged at my skirt with a special urgency. "Mommy, I want to go today. Please, Mommy, go with me." I felt really annoyed with her.

"No, Gloria, you must go down yourself. Mommy will not go with you," I told her firmly.

So the moment passed. Then a woman got

to her feet and began to thank the congregation for their prayers. As she testified about God's working in her life, I felt strangely moved by her words. Apparently Brother Wilson did too.

"Friends, I feel led to have *one more stanza* of the invitation hymn," he said.

Well, I tell you! When he said those words something hit me like a rock between the eyes. I bent down to my daughter. "Gloria, do you still want to go? Mommy will go with you."

I took her hand, but she led me. And the moment we walked out into the aisle, here came Bobby! Right behind us, independent and unafraid, our son walked alone.

During our approach to the altar, I perceived the truth: Bobby is an independent child, ready to walk out by himself. Gloria needs me to hold her hand, but her desire is just as genuine. God had to show me she needed me to go with her.

The instant Brother Claude issued that second invitation, I knew, "This is for Gloria." The Holy Spirit literally almost hit me over the head. I realized I'd been fearing what other people might think—that I was pushing my child to take this step.

Even so, I had mixed emotions. At the altar I said, "I want Bobby and Gloria to talk to a counselor without me there. I want to make sure this is genuine."

It was. Soon the three of us stood together in front of the church as other members came forward to shake out hands. I could see Bob was crying.

"This is the real thing for your children," the counselor assured me. "I talked to Bobby and Gloria. Then we prayed together. They know Jesus Christ as their Saviour. When I read Scriptures to them Gloria said, 'My Mommy and Daddy have already talked to me about that.' "

I felt tears begin to gather in my eyes as the counselor continued. "Gloria told me, 'I love Jesus and want Him to come into my heart. I want to be saved.'

"Thank God for parents like you—who influence their children toward the Christian way of life," he concluded.

"Thank you. That settles whatever doubts I had in my heart," I said. "I needed to know this is of God—not parental pushing."

Bobby and Gloria asked to be baptized that night. Bob and I really wanted Farmor and

Farfar to come down, and some of the children's friends to be there, but we decided not to wait.

"This is when the Holy Spirit is working," Bob said. "We should do it now while their desire is so strong."

Our children were baptized that same night, August 2, 1970, with just Bob and me there. This was one of the most joyous moments of our lives. We both cried like babies as we saw our babies baptized.

5 "Train Up a Child . . ."

As I write this, it's hard to realize that two years ago today Bob and I had only just turned over to Jesus something indescribably precious to us—the lives of our newborn, dying twins.

Barbara and Billy had been born two and one-half months prematurely. Together they weighed less than five pounds. When doctors told us not to hope they'd live, Bob and I faced the greatest anguish we'd ever known. Brother Bill Chapman came to my hospital room that day and helped Bob and me come to the place where we could surrender the lives of our babies into God's perfect will—no matter what His will might be.

Today Bob and I remember that act as the most difficult one in our experience. At first, in fact, it seemed impossible, but God's grace proved more than sufficient. It sustained us by means of the countless prayers of friends, strangers, even fighting men in Viet Nam, for the six desperate weeks our babies were daily in danger.

They lived, of course—but even had they not, Bob and I feel sure that in surrendering them to Jesus (and, in the process, surrendering ourselves) we could never again in our Christian lives take certain things for granted.

You might say that terrible, agonizing experience actually became the high-water mark of our Christian lives so far. At any rate, it caused us to reevaluate the direction in which we were headed as a family.

No matter how often I've shared that particular grief, surrender, joy and victory with various church groups and other audiences—always the same thing happens. I find myself weeping without restraint, as do many of my listeners.

Nor will this witness ever cease to be painful, I think. Bob and I no longer mind, however. Because of our adorable babies I've gradually become more and more willing to speak up for Christ. Tears no longer embarrass me. Bob has a deep new commitment as a Christian, a husband, and a father. And our older children—well, let's share.

Bobby was five then, Gloria just four. Both of them knew Jesus, so naturally Bob and I asked them to pray for the twins. Both children understood that our babies weren't expected to live. And did they pray! For two months they prayed so faithfully, so continuously, that Bob and I marveled. We were amazed that children so young could take on such serious responsibilities. When at last we could bring the twins home, Bobby and Gloria had the bad luck to have little colds. We had them wait inside behind glass doors while we knelt down outside, at their level, to let them see the babies.

I shall never forget the awe and delight on their faces. Their mouths were wide open. "They're so *little!*" Bobby exclaimed.

Often people ask if Bobby and Gloria are jealous of the babies. They expect us to say yes, of course, but jealousy never developed. Because they prayed so hard and had so much to do with bringing them home, there really is no resentment at all. They feel largely responsible for Billy and Barbara's being here—which they are.

No doubt that's why it's easy for them to

take their lesser problems to the Lord. Bobby and Gloria saw us ask God to work a real miracle in our lives when we prayed He'd spare our twins. They know firsthand the power of God. They remember that crisis in our lives, so they continue to depend on the Lord for other things. When either of them has a need they hop right up to the altar and pray for that need—sure He'll grant their request immediately.

Take Bobby's apprehension about tornados, for example. Maybe he'd seen us dashing around preparing for a hurricane; or maybe the *Wizard of Oz* alarmed him. Anyhow, he got very interested in tornados. He'd talk about them a lot and draw them in pictures. He didn't exactly have a complex about storms, but there was definitely some fear there. Whenever it thundered at night, he'd get scared.

"Bobby, why don't you pray about that?" Bob suggested. "Ask Jesus to take away your fear of storms." So Bobby prayed, and when a thunderstorm arrived that very night he discovered he'd lost his fears. This really impressed him.

Of course Bob and I remind our children

that God doesn't always answer prayers just the way they'd want them answered. But we believe fears like those are not from the Lord, so surely if He doesn't want us to be afraid of something as silly as a thundercloud, we have only to ask.

Mornings before school, Bob reads aloud to Bobby and Gloria from a book entitled *Little Visits With God* given to us by our dear friend Jody Dunton. It's a wonderful book of very short stories which illustrate situations children might encounter—name-calling, for example, or lying, or people who don't know how to express love. We hear one of these stories, discuss it a bit, then pray about it. This is paying off. It makes an excellent start for their day, and is teaching them in advance how best to cope with many of the little dramas that can arise in school.

Several times I've mentioned our family prayer altar. Relatively new in our home, already it's indispensable. Bob gave it to us.

The story actually began several years ago when we visited Senator and Mrs. Mark Hatfield (Mark and Antoinette) at their Washington, D.C., home. The Hatfield family is devoutly Christian. Mark and Antoinette's deep commitment to Christ impressed Bob and me from the instant we met them. And when we saw their altar—a beautiful old Early American one Mark had found at an antique shop and had restored—we felt sure this object had played an important part in their family life.

Then Antoinette told me what the altar had meant to their children, and I almost envied her a bit. "How wonderful to have a place set aside in your home," I told Bob, "a quiet place where you can draw apart and talk to God! A place established for that purpose only."

But those old altars aren't easy to find. We never seemed to run across one. We kept looking, though, because neither Bob nor I could quite forget that altar. Imagine how I felt, then, that day last summer when I ran upstairs to our bedroom for something—and there it was! Bob hadn't even given me a hint.

I simply burst into tears. Mark Hatfield had been on the lookout for such an altar ever since our last visit, it seemed. When he found one at last, he had it shipped to Bob. Bob had it refinished and repaired, then sneaked it into our room.

Soon we established our own nightly family services. Just before their bedtime, our two older children meet us at the altar which faces our fireplace. Bobby and Gloria each get to light a candle placed at either end of the mantel. They enjoy this small ceremony.

Bob reads a chapter from the Bible. Then we take turns praying—just simple little conversational prayer about whatever special things occupy our minds: thunderstorms, Gloria's close friendship with Wendy, Daddy's diet, my next performance. Afterwards, Bobby and Gloria blow out the candles. Then it's off to bed, happy and secure, all four of us feeling very close and loving.

Billy and Barbara started their bedtime prayers before they were two. Not a regular thing, but occasionally, when the time seemed right. After their baths, I'd rock them, sing to them, and tell a story. When I realized they were communicating with one another—and really understood—I tried a prayer. I was amazed to see how they stayed on their knees the whole time, placed their little hands together, and were really serious about the whole thing.

They'd blessed their food for a year before that, of course. I kept it simple so they could learn it, and of course they'd seen Bobby and Gloria pray at the table. The twins seemed to enjoy their little blessing. They say their *Amens* very heartily and loudly!

I told Bob to start coming downstairs at bedtime because the twins knew their prayers. The older children came, too, and prayed with the babies. The twins really do know the prayers. They alternate words, looking up and grinning.

Learning to pray is an integral part of their training. Actually, our babies began this training before they even were old enough for potty training. One's just as important as the other, in my opinion!

Because we want them to grow up knowing the Lord always, and because we want Him to become Master of their lives, we start very early to guide them in these simple ways. Sometimes when you're tired and cranky, it's tempting to postpone this because it takes time. But it's like disciplining a child. It's always easier to let him go his own way instead of patiently instructing him.

I wish I'd had even more training than I did

in my early life, though I was extremely fortunate in that respect. This sort of action lays a groundwork. It's as important as taking them to Sunday school, or reading to them from the Word. Bob and I believe it will be a simple transition from the nursery and the breakfast table (where the twins listen to Bob, Bobby, and Gloria discuss their *Little Visits With God*) to the family altar.

Also, even more than just training our children in what to do, we know we must live out an example before them. I just don't believe it's possible to be too strict, too firm, in establishing a foundation. The Bible says, *Train up a child in the way he should go: and . . . he will not depart from it.*

Looking back, I know I had a good foundation in the Christian life—especially from my grandparents. And from vacation Bible school. Though I knew Bible school would be good for my children, still I never dreamed it might become so directly responsible for their salvation. Bob and I still feel amazed. Maybe God blessed us because He saw the real efforts we made that week.

We could have sent our children to church instead of taking them, but I wanted *me* to be there. At least a couple of times I felt tempted to stay home and rest, but I made myself go anyhow. Odd how those were the days I came home filled with joy—how *I* was the one who received a blessing from the experience.

Oftentimes newspaper reporters, interviewing me about parental training in the Christian way, ask if I'm not afraid of overemphasizing such training in our home.

"Not at all," I tell them. "If anything, we should make it stronger in order to counteract all the other influences which can lure our children away from God."

How could we begin too young? If our tiny babies can be so in tune with things of the Lord, surely we have a responsibility to train them. "Jesus Loves the Little Children" is a song we sing at Bible school. And teaching our little ones about Him often helps Bob and me *become as a little child*, in a spiritual sense, so we can learn to better follow Him.

As God tells us in Isaiah 1:6, . . . *a little child shall lead them.*

6 Searching Questions

Debbie Malnik one of the first girls to befriend me when I moved to Miami Beach, once entered into a serious discussion with me about God and faith and believing.

"Anita, this is very easy for you to say because you're good," she protested, when I told her some of my beliefs.

"Oh, Debbie, you're so wrong!" I answered. "I'm not good. The Bible says there's no one who is good enough. There's no way you can be good enough to come into fellowship with God.

"This is His gift to us. I just have a simple faith, and accept this gift from Him. It has nothing to do with my being good, bad, or what. We're all sinners, and we have to realize that."

I shall never forget Debbie. Not only was she quick to offer her friendship, but later she was to do a very meaningful thing for our family's sake. When our twins began their long fight for survival, Debbie got down on her knees and prayed for them. Later she told me this was the first time she had prayed since childhood.

You can imagine how that touched my heart. And if it meant so very much to Bob and me, how much more it probably meant to God Himself! The marvelous thing was, Debbie's prayer was entirely unselfish. Her plea to God was in our behalf and not her own.

Good? I don't know why Debbie called *me* that!

In Ephesians 2:8, 9, Paul writes: *For by grace are ye saved through faith; and that not of yourselves: it is the gift of God: Not of works, lest any man should boast.*

Recently another friend asked me if my faith in God ever has been so severely shaken that I came close to losing it.

Yes. My faith is far from perfect. I admit there have been times in my life when, through lack of faith, I felt God had failed me. I would pray for a sin of mine, wanting Him to take it from me, yet not willing within myself to give it up. God, knowing me so well, allowed me to feel the pain of this even as I impatiently turned my back on Him.

Also there have been times in my life when I was just not myself—times I wondered if there were even a shred of godliness left in me. I was tempted, and struggling for my soul. I really thought I was going to lose it.

At one time I was having such difficulties in my marriage and in other human relationships, and got so weary of my own sinfulness, that I felt strongly tempted to sever with God. Yet something made me hang on. I know that must have been God within me.

I shudder to remember that time in my life. Not just because I nearly—through my sinfulness—lost my husband and marriage, but also because in my torment of willfulness and wrong thinking, I nearly separated myself from my God.

No, I really don't have it made as a Christian—nor do I ever expect to. Through the grace of God, however, our home today is happy and secure as we attempt to live the Christian life. Yet I know from experience that's when Satan is most likely to step in and create fears and dissatisfactions—or to use one of his favorite tools: discouragement.

(Okay, Bob. You said to tell it like it is!)

Perhaps a lot of what I've told so far simply sounds too easy—as if I can just pick up the phone, ring up God, and tell Him what I'd like Him to do. That's far from the case, though there have been some real victories lately. I thank God for these.

But something else is happening to me these days—something I can't analyze. It's as though the Lord has been shaking me up lately, preparing me for something, and—well, here's the truth. I seem reluctant to get with it. Sometimes I act like a rebellious child.

Why? For one thing, I'm too happy. That's right! Bob says nobody else in the world but me would ever have the nerve to complain she was too happy, and that's probably true. But even as a child I was like that. If anything good happened to me I couldn't accept it. Afterwards I'd go into a terrific depression which would strip away the joy.

Today there are times when I experience perfect joy—with the children, with Bob, with certain victories God sends to our lives. But this never lasts, because I'm afraid everything is so perfect it *can't* last. We're so abundantly blessed, and I know I'm not worthy of it. So emotionally I'm either way up or way down.

Okay. Of course I know this is all wrong. My attitude—which is all too human—simply indicates a lack of faith. The Bible tells us that perfect love casts out fear. When I can learn to love and trust God more—*really* love Him—I won't fear losing the blessings He showers on us.

He's simply going to have to change the fearful, pessimistic streak in me. I'm going to have to become willing to let Him change it. However, though I know I'm broken to some extent, I also know I'm not yet willing to be totally yielded. Why do we struggle so against allowing our human natures to be changed?

Then too, like many another woman in America today, I seem to want to be able to eat my cake and still have it. For example, sometimes I envy my wealthy women friends who married into the kind of life they lead, instead of having to work. But would I swap places with them?

Not really. Among these women who don't have to do a blessed thing I can see a lot of discontent and unfulfillment. Too often I can see obvious lacks in their marriages, as well.

On the other hand, I know God has given me a real calling. He blesses our efforts beyond our wildest expectations, and gives us satisfactions beyond telling. I know I really don't choose to lead an idle life. So why am I so perverse?

Then there's the problem of materialism. Jesus tells us how hard it is for a rich man to enter the kingdom of heaven. Most of us think that's a problem we'll never have to face—and then we wake up one morning, worrying, and realize how much store we set by certain material things. Our beautiful home, in my case. Private schools for the children. Even the pleasure of dressing them in cute clothes—a compensation, I realize, for the hand-me-downs I often wore as a child.

Now none of these in themselves are evil. But could I eventually begin to place these first in my life? Would I be willing to give up our present style of living if God led us into something simpler? And what if we lost all our worldly possessions? Then would I honestly claim my God would be sufficient?

I know He would. But could I really accept His will for me if it ran so contrary to my own? Not too gracefully, I'm afraid, if I know myself at all! I know it's time I became more yielding to my Lord, but I'm afraid of what He may ask me to give up. In many ways our life at this moment seems so perfect. . . .

Bob describes the Christian life as that of attaining a series of plateaus. I don't know whether I'm about to arrive at a new stage of my own Christian experience, or trying hard not to!

There are two things at the root of my present rebellion. One is Bob's continual insistence that I give my Christian witness. I believe Bob somehow feels he's witnessing, through me. The other is my own desire for Bob to assume more the spiritual leadership of our home.

My husband continues to think of himself as a new Christian, though he's in his eleventh year in the Christian life. And why isn't Bob more the spiritual head of our family? Part of my turmoil arises from the fact that I'm really ready to go deeper into Christian commitment—yet I'm not willing to go alone.

So many other wives share this complaint. You hear it all the time. And there really is no other frustration quite like the longing to become more seriously involved in the Christian life, yet not wanting to until one's husband is ready. What is the answer for women like me?

As for witnessing—this is an old battle. Bob knows how difficult this always has been for me. It's a case of having to strip away your ego completely, to lay your soul bare for the Lord.

There may be only a little time left in which we can speak up for Jesus, yet I feel a lack within myself. I feel so inadequate and limited, partly, I realize, because I really don't know the Bible sufficiently well. Yet Bob continues to exhort me to share my Christian testimony, no matter how difficult this may be for me. And my heart also tells me I must share Jesus, even when my courage fails me.

I think back to the Christmas holidays when I visited Dan Topping, our family friend, in the hospital. For two years I've felt a burden for Dan who has been in very poor health. That day, during our visit, there came a perfect opportunity for me to urge Dan to let Christ help him.

But I just couldn't do it. I looked at our successful and sophisticated friend, who is a bit older than I and quite a bit more worldly—and I lost my nerve.

Closer to home, there's Farfar and Farmor.

What is our duty to them?

"How do we reach your parents?" I asked Bob.

"I can't. You're going to have to do it," he said. Then I really got belligerent. I figure they'd really listen to their only son whom they love so dearly, but instead he fluffs it off on me—which is a cop-out. Doesn't Bob see why I can't do it? I'd never want Farfar and Farmor to think I don't love them as they are—that they must come to God before they'd be good enough to suit me!

Of course, the hardest place in the world to witness is in your own home: to one's husband or child, parent or in-law. Once again, it's a case of loving God more than one's self.

What next?

I don't know, nor do I feel like thrashing these matters out with Bob. At the moment I'm praying about them, trying to bring resentments under control and rid myself of childish fears, and, hardest of all, trying to will to do God's will.

As I ponder these rather immature problems I can only smile to think Debbie once called me *good*. No, Debbie. But God is good, even if I'm not.

Certainly all my blessings—Bob and the babies—the many deep satisfactions our Christian life brings us—the good things our profession provides—all this is God-given, not anything I ever earned or deserved.

I remind myself too that most of the good things in my life are gifts I never dreamed of receiving.

Yet God meant them for me.

7   Bob's Diet

"I think we ought to talk about the time prayer didn't work," Bob said.

"Okay, Bob. Now it's your turn to tell it like it is," I challenged him.

"Anita, you've got a wicked gleam in your eye. This may sound funny to you, but to me it's pretty serious. You find out just how weak you really are when you try to diet. Suddenly I have great compassion for people who try to stop smoking. Giving up drugs must be almost impossible!"

"If you really want to lose weight, start sitting between the twins at the dinner table," I suggested. "It's like refereeing a tennis match. Who has time to eat?"

Bob didn't think much of that suggestion, I could tell. I hurried on. "So describe the diet bit, then, even if it makes you feel silly. After all, so often it's the little things that trip us Christians up—not the big hurdles, but the

73

tiny things that make up our lives.''

"Right. Well, I've been fighting this diet a long time. Every so often I'd talk to myself, 'Look. The only way you can get strength is through Christ, right?' So I'd really pray about it.

"I'd put notes on the refrigerator: JESUS IS WATCHING YOU. JESUS THINKS YOU'RE A FAT SLOB. And the kids prayed for me. At night they'd say, 'God bless Mommy and Daddy, and help Daddy stay on his diet.' I had all these great things going for me.

"So then I'd even say a prayer, *Jesus, don't let me open the refrigerator door*—even as I opened it! And I'd see the remains of a birthday cake in the freezer and say, *Dear God, don't let me be tempted by it.* Then I'd attack it and fill my face.

"After I had a full stomach I'd feel disgraced. I'd say, *My God, I've let my children down. What kind of person am I?*''

By then I couldn't help smiling at Bob. But he looked very serious and sincere, so I listened. "Overeating, so far as I'm concerned, is abusing your body," he explained.

"When I'm sinning, I'm fat. But I'm not

perfect. I am a sinner, and I have to pick myself up and keep trying. I'm very, very down on myself because I didn't have enough self-control to do it on my own. It's ridiculous—really dumb.''

How surprising. Bob's not all that overweight, after all. I had no idea he felt such a sense of shame about it!

"So that's where our friend, Dr. Bernie Vinoski, came in," Bob said. "He prescribed some pills and said, 'Take these until you start losing weight and get into the correct eating patterns. Then get off the pills and everything will be all right.'

"Our Lord said we have to come as a little child, and with these pills I really feel childish. It would have been a lot better if I could have done it with Christ instead of with pills, but I guess I'm just not ready yet.''

"Not ready? Bob, you know better than that," I had to protest.

"You've got to handle the Christian life according to the kind of person you are," he argued. "Some of us grow slowly. Some react as though struck by a bolt of lightning. I think it's important to realize that God knows you and deals with the person He knows, in the

75

way that's best and most reasonable for that individual.

"In my own case, coming to Christianity from show business when I was nearly thirty, I had a lot of cynical attitudes and plenty of skepticism to strip away. I had put up barriers and defenses in my life, and these had to go. The stripping-away process comes hard for some of us. In my case it's still going on."

We fell silent for a moment. Then another, more alarming question occurred to me. "Bob, do you think your conversion was an emotional experience?"

"Partly. We were about to get married. I was really very ignorant about Christianity then, and I'm sure it was an emotional thing. I see people making the decision to accept Christ as their personal Saviour, and they never again, ever, follow up on this. This must be just an emotion, I think, and not a genuine conversion.

"Actually, I'm convinced we have to have many 'conversions' as we move from stage to stage in our Christian lives. This is part of growing as a Christian," he explained.

"Bob, has all this been pretty hard for you?"

"Sure. That's why I care so much that the Christian outlook be instilled in our children early. If we waited until they were twenty it would be a lot of work. Hard work. I'm becoming a great fan of family worship. I see the results. I really wish I'd had this kind of training in my childhood, Anita.

"You see, I believe in stages. It doesn't seem logical to me to expect a person who has rocked along forever with no knowledge of Christ to come to a decision in a little church somewhere and—pow—just like that he's a perfect Christian. I believe you have to work at it, and there are definite stages of growth."

"Bob, you've been a Christian for more than ten years now."

"You might say that. Actually, the first several years of our marriage was so tumultuous that I'd have to say I've probably only been a practicing, consistent Christian for five or maybe six years.

"The twins. Their problems presented the biggest test I've faced so far as a Christian. But I really did put them in God's hands, and I know I would not have blamed God if they had died. That represents definite new growth for me as a Christian."

"Do you ever doubt any more, Bob?" I asked, curious.

"Sure. We all have our doubts. I think this comes from our looking towards man as an example. Man will let you down every time. How often we say, 'Gee, he's a preacher. He ought to be pretty great, yet . . .' But that's man. Nothing man does should cause us to turn down our faith. Christ will never fail us."

Well! In Luke 11:9, Jesus tells us, *Ask, and it shall be given you.* . . . I only expected Bob to tell about his diet, but he has gone on to share his ideas about the care and feeding of the new Christian!

He groped for words. "I'm like a premature baby. I'm a babe in Christ, small at first, then catching up—sometimes slowly—sometimes in big leaps.

"It was your idea that we all worship together, Anita. If you hadn't felt the need for these practices I probably never would have suggested them. But now I'm a firm believer."

Yes, and it was Bob who bought the altar.

"Anita, I realize I'm not the spiritual leader in this house the way I should be." I stared at Bob, amazed.

"I guess I could be. I could fake it. But I don't want that. There's nothing wrong with you being ahead of me spiritually. You're the one who has led me this far. I have to grow at my own rate," he said quietly. "Life in Christ simply cannot be hurried or pushed. I can't always come to an immediate decision—even if Anita Bryant does get upset with me!"

8 Amazing Grace

"Anita, would you sing at my funeral?"

The question stunned me, but Aunt Berthie's eyes looked straight into mine. I had to answer.

"Of course, Aunt Berthie," I stammered. "I'd be glad to . . . I mean, I really don't know if I can, but I'll try."

"Sure you can, Honey," Aunt Berthie said in her matter-of-fact way. She placed her hand over mine to comfort me. The sight of that hand, now transparent as a leaf, made sorrow rise in my chest.

"Here's what I want you to sing," she said. " 'How Great Thou Art,' for one thing. And of course my all-time favorite, 'Amazing Grace.' "

I could only nod, too shocked to speak. I didn't know you could talk about your own dying—that you could actually plan your funeral!

But I was just a twenty-year-old bride that day more than ten years ago at Aunt Berthie's bedside. Today a phone call from Marabel Morgan made me start thinking about Aunt Berthie and some other extraordinary people in my life. All this because Marabel is teaching in her home a course entitled "Total Woman," using the Bible as her textbook.

"Total Woman." I find myself thinking about certain women—and men—who, by their examples, have inspired me to reach toward full womanhood.

You'd need to know Bertha Berry Adkinson, my mother's remarkable older sister, to understand what really happened between us that day at her deathbed. In fact, it's only now I realize Aunt Berthie made that request for my sake, not her own.

She knew I'd never seen anything of death firsthand. So in her practical way, Aunt Berthie intended to see that I didn't surround the fact of death with any unnecessary fears or nonsense. She had been dying of cancer, after all, for five years. Everybody knew that.

For her, those were witnessing years. She

went to church faithfully, even when the pain got so bad she'd have to recline on a sofa at the back of the sanctuary. On good days she'd invite a young neighbor to share her lunch of green beans and cornbread, and share their victories in the Lord, as well. Or she'd offer to baby-sit so some young mother could rest for a bit.

When the pain got very bad, Aunt Berthie learned to relax through prayer. She told some people she'd really like to die, but felt sure God wanted her to hang on a little longer for her daughters' sakes: Marilyn, still a teen-ager, and Gigi, a young wife and mother.

When I got word the end was near, I flew to Aunt Berthie's home in Odessa, Texas. What I saw that day shocked me, and she knew it. The sight of a once large, outgoing woman now reduced to a feeble, living skeleton who weighed less than one hundred pounds—the pervasive sickroom odor, the terrible inevitability of death—all this left me at a loss for words. Typically, Aunt Berthie ended up comforting *me*.

The physical contrast between us must have been dramatic enough. Aunt Berthie weak, emaciated and nearly consumed by pain—I young and healthy, a happy newlywed who looked and felt terribly out of place in the awful presence of such suffering.

The real contrast between us, however, was in spirit. Mine was young and untested, fearful at the thought of anything so alien as death. Hers was the bright, brave one, full of Christian confidence and still so eager to give. love and reassure. She gave me so very much that day.

Soon Aunt Berthie died, and I did sing at her funeral. It seemed hard, but I told myself, This is for Aunt Berthie. If she could have the faith she did, this is the least I can do.

Ignorant as I was about death, her approach to eternal life both inspired and intimidated me. "She's a tower of strength," I told Bob. "I just hope I could die exhibiting that kind of Christian faith."

Inside myself, I certainly doubted it. People who knew Aunt Berthie still speak of her as a model of courage, serenity, and the kind of graceful acceptance of facts that let her keep her great sense of humor to the last.

"My insurance company and I paid for that new wing on the Odessa Memorial Hospital," she joked after her fifth major operation in four years.

At that time I thought Aunt Berthie was teaching us all how to die. Now I realize that frail, wasted, yet thoroughly triumphant woman taught us something infinitely more important.

Not how to die—not that at all—but how to *live*.

What makes some individuals so strong? Where does a faith like Aunt Berthie's come from? I believe that sort of strength of character has to be caught rather than taught.

Both of my parents came from large, old-fashioned pioneer families in rural Oklahoma. Sandra and I grew up surrounded by strong, colorful kinfolk. A child recognizes and admires real character, I'm sure. At any rate, I grew up thinking of certain relatives as being just naturally strong and sanctified types—quite different from me.

Take Grandpa and Grandma Berry. Grandma probably was the strongest influence on my life. She was my model of an ideal woman. Married at fifteen, illiterate until Grandpa taught her to read and write, Grandma gave birth to nine sons and daughters in their big old country house in Barnsdall, Oklahoma.

What made Grandma Berry seem so special to me? She simply was the most loving, giving Christian I ever knew. Her faith remained radiant and unshakable. I never saw her lose her temper, never heard her complain. And when Grandpa Berry was blinded in a tragic oil field accident, she simply took over and made do. Somehow she took care of him in addition to all the others, helped him raise a garden, kept him from ever giving up.

Grandpa Berry, who was saved in the hospital, always wept to speak of his salvation. "I had to go through the pain and suffering of having my eyes put out before I could see," he tells people. At times I guess he has embarrassed every member of his family because he'll walk up to a stranger and ask, "Do you know Jesus Christ as your Lord and Saviour?" He doesn't even introduce himself first!

But God is so real to Grandpa that he just has to witness. He feels he wasted so many years not living for the Lord that now he wants to tell everybody he meets about Him.

My father's parents also were faithful

church people. Grandpa and Grandma Bryant raised Daddy as a Christian. He attended the Church of Christ in Sasakwa, Oklahoma.

I'm built a lot like Grandma Bryant, and I suspect I also inherited her hot temper. She was a tiny little woman, with coal-black hair that hung below her waist, all pulled up in a knot atop her little head. She was a hard-working pioneer type.

Grandpa Bryant—a warm, outgoing giant of a man—was half Cherokee Indian. He used to hold Sandra and me on his lap and tell us Indian stories. We loved to hear Grandpa (who was a great storyteller) recount adventure tales in his rich, deep voice.

Daddy and Mother (who married right after they graduated from high school) divorced just before Sandra and I became teen-agers. Young as they were when we were born, however, our parents nevertheless trained Sandra and me carefully. They had come from good, strict homes, and they passed along the high standards and good values they'd received.

When I was eight Daddy decided to leave his job as an oil field roustabout and strike out for Midwest City, a suburb of Oklahoma City, so Sandra and I could have extra advantages.

He thought we had talents which deserved training.

Now that I'm grown, I see what a brave thing that was for a young father to do—especially considering he had to take a half cut in pay. Because Daddy made that sacrifice, I received the singing and dancing lessons, the early radio and television experience that led directly into my career.

I wonder what gave Daddy so much faith in our potential. Though Sandra didn't become a professional performer, she could have. She's a beautiful dancer. Anyhow, Daddy and Mother really sacrificed for us. That's the kind of faith you seem to absorb through your pores—the unselfish faith of your parents.

Mother must have been just about my present age when she was left alone to raise two girls. Despite all the hard work and privation, we never heard her complain. She's too much like Grandma Berry to complain, I guess.

And though Mother's life was far from easy, it never occurred to her that God would not see her through anything she had to face. She had been raised to rely on God—and that's what she did.

"I've wandered away from my faith at times, but never completely," she told me. "I couldn't have made it without God. Every night I prayed for guidance so I'd know how to raise you and Sandra right. Somehow I knew God would bring us through."

He did, Mother. He really did!

Once Mother remarked on Grandma Berry's faith. "It wasn't something she talked about, but something she lived," Mother said. "It sure showed when Bertha was so ill. She helped Bertha all she could, and she never broke down. And when the end came, she simply said, *Thank you, Lord.* She was that glad to see her daughter free of suffering." Then Mother went on to say something very poignant and revealing. "I've often wondered if I could be that unselfish. It would be very hard to give up one of my children. The thing is, she *knew* Bertha went to be with God in heaven."

Today the world seems so much more sophisticated and so much less solid than all that, somehow. It's hard these days to hold on to the sturdy values by which our rural forebears lived their lives. Certainly Miami Beach and show business seem about as far away as one can get from that sort of simplicity and goodness.

That's one reason I'm so grateful that our children have Farmor and Farfar Green to give them the special sort of patience and stability that only grandparents seem to possess. Farmor and Farfar also are pioneer types, but in a European way. When they first came to America they lived in New York City in the Bronx, and life was very hard. Farmor had to scrimp and save always. They lived up five flights of stairs. And Farmor walked five miles to the hospital to have Bob.

I admire Farmor so much, and Bob is so much like her—a strong person who basically is the world's softest touch. Farmor gets down and plays games with the babies. She has a lot of patience with young children.

But Bob also is a lot like Farfar. My father-in-law is a very gentle man, somewhat shy but with great personal warmth. One thing I love about him is the fact that he loves to hear the choir in our church. I certainly relate to that!

Now that I've entered my thirties, it's time to seek deeper values for my own life as well as consciously trying to help my children establish strong foundations for their own Christian lives.

You think of people like your grandparents and others (people you've considered from childhood to be supermen and women). And then, from out of the blue, it comes as a jolt to learn that these extraordinary men and women maybe had some of the same very ordinary fears and hangups which bug me today.

I recall Grandma Berry when she came to visit Farmor and Farfar Green in Florida at Boynton Beach a few years ago. To my complete astonishment, Grandpa warned Bob's parents not to worry if they heard noises in the night—that Grandma sometimes had bad dreams.

My Grandma Berry! The strongest woman in the world?

You grow up holding a certain image of your grandma. Then you discover she has nightmares sometimes, and cries out, and even walks in her sleep!

It's time I began to put away some of the hero worship and start to think of Grandma Berry more realistically. She must have had great fears and insecurities beneath that perfectly controlled exterior. In fact, I'm beginning to see she may have been as big a bundle of complexities as I sometimes am!

When I asked Gigi to recall what she could for me about her mother, my Aunt Berthie, she told how Aunt Berthie often would weep with pain and discouragement—but dry her tears the moment anyone came into her room, and begin to witness to them.

Do you suppose I feel disillusioned to learn that these towering Christians actually had some very human fears and setbacks? Not at all. Rather, it's great to discover that they, too, had to get in there and grapple with their weaknesses.

I grew up knowing the important fact of their faith in God. Now I'm beginning to see something else equally important: that only through claiming God's ever-present grace and mercy can even the strongest Christian sustain his faith.

God's amazing grace.

Who could pretend to comprehend it?

Whenever I think of Aunt Berthie's inspiring Christian faith, I'll be bound to remember the day she asked me to sing "Amazing Grace."

I feel confident Aunt Berthie knew the

Eternal Source of all faith and all grace. And she helped me, too, to know.

9   Come as a Little Child

I tiptoed into my Sunday school class, somewhat late. Pat Phillips, our class president, was praying. She didn't see me slip in.

". . . and dear Lord, be with Anita as she travels, and watch over her," she prayed. "We thank You that she loves Jesus, and is not afraid to take a stand for Him."

I felt very deeply touched and grateful.

Then Pat opened her eyes and saw me. "Dear Lord, my prayer already is answered!" she exclaimed.

We all had a good laugh over that. But it's more than just a funny little event; it's also something of a parable. Sometimes God seems to answer our prayers almost faster than we can voice them.

"Pray about it, Anita," Bob had advised me that afternoon a month ago—the day this book began.

I did pray, of course. And looking back now, I can see that even as Bob and I talked that day, God already had set in motion His wonderful design for our next weeks.

That night Mary came to Christ. What a blessing it is to have under your roof a person newly committed to our Lord! The difficult circumstances in Mary's life did not change—but she did.

As we observed her faith and confidence increase, her conversion experience spilled over onto other members of our household. And I needed some spillover! My own internal struggles had begun to take their toll.

There were moments when life at Villa Verde seemed almost unbearably sweet: Gloria Lynn showing us her new ballet steps—Bob and Bobby shouting with excitement as they watch the televised splashdown of our country's Apollo 14 astronauts—taking the babies into the pool for our own splashdown.

"I can't bear to miss a minute with our children," I told Bob. "Each one is so precious. And babyhood slips away so terribly fast."

As usual, the beauty at this point in our lives

served to depress me. How can this last? I asked myself time and again.

It can't last, of course. Hebrews 13:8 tells us, *Jesus Christ the same yesterday, and to day, and for ever.* But only He remains the same; the rest of us must be born again, and each of us must grow in grace and in knowledge of the Lord Jesus.

Mary's new commitment made me yearn to know God's will for my life. I made serious attempts to give over into His hands all my inner conflicts, yet somehow I seemed to receive no clear answer.

It's hard sometimes just to wait upon the Lord. Wait and pray. *Pray for the book. Pray to know God's will. Pray to yield my stubborn nature, my impatience, my resistance.*

"Putting things down on paper this way is great for summing up what you really believe," Bob remarked once. "You're going to make some interesting discoveries about your faith."

"Oh yeah?" I replied rather skeptically. "I'm beginning to wonder if it's coming unglued."

I had told Mary she must come to God as a little child. One day, thinking about that piece of advice, I suddenly saw it didn't jibe with *my* approach.

"I get discouraged about my faith because I'm striving too hard for perfection," I told Bob. "No wonder I feel like such a failure most of the time. I want the kind of faith that can move great mountains when what I need to do is begin to take each day a step at a time."

"Right, Anita!" he encouraged me. "If we'd just begin our day by praying something as simple as *Lord, take me through this day.* That's really all the faith you need—just enough to know God will get you through one day.

"To have the love of God in your heart—to want to try and be like Jesus—to touch everyone you meet that day, and show them in some way you are concerned for their souls—*that's* what faith is all about."

Stages. Bob realizes faith must grow one step at a time. He knows it's much better to start the day simply praying that prayer—and meaning it—than to build up gigantic expectations which the devil can undermine.

So I, like Mary, tried to become as a little child. I saw my faith must become simpler, more consistent, more of a day-to-day effort in my home. What need to worry about the souls I might reach at the Billy Graham Crusades, the Oral Roberts television appearances, and others, in the books I write—if I don't live my faith in the small ways in the nitty-gritty of life?

Instead, I'll worry about . . . .

Why, *don't* worry! Just lay your burden before the Lord! That worry is taking up energy that God could put to better use. It's being wasted. And basically, I'm a worrier.

Think of all the years you've wasted agitating about things when you could have put that effort to much better use, I scolded myself. From now on I won't hassle about moving great mountains. I'm just going to take each day as it comes and try to be a witness.

Look at each day, each situation, each person you meet, I told myself. What can you say to help this person come to know Christ? What will strengthen his faith, if he already believes? Or what can you do for someone else to help him get through his day?

I've always been such a dreamer. Dreamed of doing such great things, and overlooked some of the first, simple, important steps.

Yes, I must go back. I must become as a little child.

So I returned to Bob's Stage One in my prayers. *Lord, help me through this day.* Soon it seemed right to add, *Lord, today help me find someone with a special need. Maybe I can help meet that need, or minister to them in some special way.*

Let me warn you! Don't ever pray anything unless you mean it. Prayers like that one have a way of getting answered much more speedily than you intended, as I quickly discovered.

Someone with a special need? I found him at a luncheon Bob and I attended. My *someone* turned out to be the guest of honor!

Bill (as I'll call him) is a distinguished and well-to-do businessman with whom Bob and I enjoyed a good working relationship. He is old enough to be my father. Neither Bob nor I ever had talked to him in any really personal way, but a week earlier we'd heard talk that personal problems had led Bill to the point of threatening suicide.

Bob and I felt great concern for him. I phoned Bill and asked if he'd meet me just before the luncheon, but I didn't tell him why.

Then I telephoned Brother Bill Chapman and asked him to arm me with Scriptures to use in helping this man.

"He . . . has an alcohol problem . . . ," I began.

"Anita, give your friend these passages from God's Word. Read them, pray over them, and then read them to him," he encouraged me. "I suggest you use Luke 12:15–21; John 3:1–16; First Corinthians 6:9–11 and Romans 10:9–10, 13. I'll be praying for you."

It was a very nervous but determined Anita who met with Bill and his wife in their motel room several days later. The Bible I carried had markers to help me find those verses quickly, and I lost no time in reading them to my friend in the order Brother Bill had suggested.

God's Word convicted Bill. I shall never forget how he listened to the story of Nicodemus, and the look on his face as he heard Jesus' words, *Verily, verily, I say unto thee, Except a man be born again, he cannot see the kingdom of God.*

At last Bill, his wife and I went down on our knees and he prayed the prayer of salvation. I wept to hear this man say, "Jesus, come into my heart."

"Bob, I still can't quite believe it!" I marveled. My emotions spilled over as I shared what happened to Bill while Bob drove us home.

"It was nothing like with Mary. I didn't hesitate a moment. Didn't have time to be scared, really. It was as if the Holy Spirit gave me a shove in Bill's direction and said, 'Go!' But now it's over, I'm scared to death!"

"Scared?"

"Sure. He's so much older than I—smart and successful and all those things. If I'd stopped and thought, I couldn't have done it, Bob. He's just not the kind of person I can witness to."

"But you did. And if you could tell Bill about Jesus, I guess you could talk to Dan."

I simply stared at him. So Bob knew how increasingly burdened I'd become for Dan Topping.

"Oh, Bob! Remember last summer at the Billy Graham Crusade? I so much hoped Dan would come to the Lord that night."

(. . . On the opening night of Evangelist Billy Graham's New York Crusade, I'd been privileged to sing and give my personal testimony for the Lord. My dear friend Gloria Roe, one of the country's foremost composers, played for me! Some 35,000 Americans packed Shea Stadium that evening. I prayed mightily before witnessing.

It wasn't the crowd. I've sung to audiences that size a number of times. It's that when I witness I'm so unworthy, so wretched, so ungodlike, that in order to become a vehicle God can use, I have to strip Anita Bryant away.

When I perform, I come on like Gangbusters, and all that ego is there. But when I come forward to testify for Christ, Anita Bryant the performer must be put aside.

It frightens me to reveal my inner self so wholeheartedly I literally quake inside. I know I have nothing to offer. What's more, the process of putting self aside can be almost agonizingly difficult, because as a performer, all my life, self has been fed.

That night I not only prayed the Lord would use my testimony, but I also prayed that seven of our Miami Beach friends in the congregation—Dan and Charlotte Topping, their four young sons and one small daughter—might experience a miracle. . . .)

Bob and I were quiet now, remembering.

"Anita, it really wasn't Dan so much that night, was it?" Bob asked thoughtfully. "I seem to remember you felt burdened, for Charlotte then—that you felt *she* was seeking the Lord."

Suddenly something clicked. "That's right, Bob! I guess I thought there was a big chance Charlotte would find Jesus, but Dan wasn't especially looking."

I felt a great surge of excitement.

"Bob, do you suppose that's why I can't bring myself to speak to Dan? Maybe the Lord wants me to talk to Charlotte first!"

Inside I felt the kind of elation that comes when you stumble onto something that seems very, very right. Bob didn't seem to respond, however.

"Maybe that's it, Anita," he said slowly. "But remember, the Lord has His own perfect timetable. Don't try to stampede Him on this thing."

Suddenly we both kind of laughed at

his warning.

Me stampede? Me, the gal who's so scared to witness? My, how things have changed!

10 Born Again

"You've been born again, Bill. It's true that all things are new to you now. But your heart can tell you one thing and your body—with all its old habits—doesn't yet live by what the heart says to do."

I'd never dreamed that witnessing could be such hard work. The first thrill of Bill's conversion had left him. Now reality—the cold, hard facts of life as he always had known it—had begun to return.

Only a few days earlier Bill had knelt and confessed Jesus Christ as his personal Saviour. But now what? Must I convince him all over again?

"It takes time for any of us to really do a turnabout in many of our habits," I told our friend. "You have the desire, but it won't happen just like that—just because you said you accepted Christ in your life.

"The Christian life is the most difficult way

to live. Trouble is, most of us Christians really don't tell it like it is: that you are new, with a fresh start, a clean slate, a new chance—but no guarantee you won't fall into deep holes, or that it ever will become easy.

"This life may be even harder than your old life. I think that's why many new Christians fail—because they don't expect this. These facts are glossed over by so many other Christians, so the new believer has a real jolt in store for him.

" 'Accept Christ and that's it,' so many of us tell the unbeliever. That's *not* it. Life is not like that."

I felt extremely discouraged. Bill had gotten pretty drunk, then telephoned me. Not only was I dismayed and unprepared, but I couldn't seem to read him. Was he sorry about his commitment—or merely fearful?

Bill sounded uncertain. "I . . . don't know if I can do it," he said at last.

"Why not, Bill?"

"I don't know how," he said, simply.

I took a deep breath and prayed a little prayer for God's guidance. What do you tell a new babe in Christ? What would Bob advise him? I took a long look at Bill—really tried to see the person inside as God saw him: a newborn Christian, shy, uncertain, a little frightened.

But how did Bill see himself? Approaching sixty. Successful, by the world's standards. Well-to-do. A definite alcohol problem. Someone who had just taken an unexpected step—a leap of faith—but wasn't sure, now, that he had the energy to venture further.

"Oh, Bill, you can do it, with God's help!" I blurted out.

"What do you suggest, Anita?"

"What would I advise a babe in Christ? To stay as close to God, to His Word, and to Christ as you can in everything, continually praying to the Lord with every move you make, lest you fall.

"And you will. The devil works overtime against the new Christian. It makes him terribly unhappy to see a soul drawn to Jesus."

Bill laughed. "Do you actually believe there's a devil?"

"Of course I do. Jesus faced the devil and overcame him. Read Matthew 4:10–11, where Jesus says, *Get thee hence, Satan.* Read Mark 1:13. The devil tries to undermine me the very instant I make a new commitment to God. It happens every time. It's very frustrating, Bill, but you can't give up. God won't let you.

"Just don't expect all miracles the first day. Take it a little at a time. But be sure to feed yourself and to grow in the Word. Read the New Testament, in particular. Let Jesus teach you."

Bill was listening intently now. I hesitated before broaching the next subject. "Do you attend church, Bill?"

"Well, we belong to a church. But you know how it is. We get there when we can, but somehow. . . ."

"Nope. That won't do," I told him firmly.

"Find a church where the Holy Spirit exists, and the preacher preaches God's Word and not the 'social gospel.' Know this beyond a shadow of a doubt, and pray hard before you join that church.

"Bill, you're going to have to take on the responsibility of placing yourself where you know God wants you to be. When a baby is born, he needs people to nurture and love him. You are a babe in Christ, and you desperately need this loving care.

"Fail to give an infant food and water, and

he'll perish. This happens to the new Christian too, Bill, if he doesn't have fellowship and the Word which is his spiritual food.''

We were silent for a moment. Would Bill reject my suggestions? Did they seem too simplistic for him?

"Read my Bible and go to church," he repeated. "What else? Is that all I have to do to become a good Christian?"

"*Pray,*" I told him, fervently. "Remember, your old sins have been forgiven. You now can make a fresh start in life. Still, you have no guarantee you'll achieve your spiritual potential—and you really won't—unless you make up your mind to seek it, with faith.

"My own biggest problem is that I get impatient," I confessed. "I want *success* as a Christian right now. I keep asking why I have to go through this, make that mistake, fall down and pick myself up.

"Why, I ask myself, if God made me with this mind and this body, did He not make me naturally better? Why do I have to learn all these hard lessons?"

Bill seemed somewhat unconvinced as I explained that these rebellious questions continue to come up—even with old Christians. "It's the devil," I told him. "You'll have to fight him every step of the way."

Particularly when you have a stubborn nature like mine, I thought. Or maybe an alcohol problem. . . . Wish Bob were here. A man could talk to Bill about the drinking better than I could. I couldn't talk about that.

But those were my ideas, not the Holy Spirit's. Again I read First Corinthians 6:9–11 to Bill. Then I turned to First Peter 5:6–7, and these verses had an impact on me as well as Bill. Suddenly and forcefully, I began to speak to my friend from the bottom of my heart. All my self-consciousness vanished. My one desire was that he might know God's power and grace and mercy. I felt free—I saw with great amazement—free to speak without embarrassment, certain God was using me as His vehicle to bring the message to His new babe.

"Doctors say drunkenness is a sickness, but God calls it a sin. Ask Jesus to help you. Give up alcohol today," I begged him.

"I can't!" he almost whispered.

"Yes, you can. You have Christ on your

112

side now, Bill. You know, my very favorite verse in all the Bible is Philippians 4:13: *I can do all things through Christ, which strengtheneth me.*"

"Claim that promise," I pleaded. "Remember, once the devil gets a foothold inside the door of your life, you're at a very dangerous place indeed.

"Temptations! If you yield to that first one, it's like a little leak. The others quickly flood in behind it, and you can't do much about them. You're knocked flat—going under—knowing you're unable to save yourself.

"Still, if you can manage even to whisper *God help me*—and mean it—He can and will save you. From yourself. From the evils inside you, and those outside in the world. Just that little *God help me* makes the difference."

And that was so true, I thought, as I prepared to send Bill the new *Scofield Reference Bible* Bob and I had chosen for his conversion gift.

Today the devil tried to convince me I couldn't witness to you. I believed I would become paralyzed with shyness and downright fear. Bill, I could hardly even pray for you.

Still, that little *God help me!* was enough—enough to overthrow all the wiles, all the power of the devil. Then God could let me witness!

11   God's Business

"Well, I don't go any further," I told our audience. "I'm a Southern Baptist—and you *know* I ain't gonna go any further."

That line always gets a laugh. You see, the transition from pop songs into the country and Western segment of our show calls for a quick costume change.

It's *mighty* quick, like about thirty seconds. I simply waltz offstage, put on boots and a Western hat, and strut right back on. Then I take off my fancy skirt—and there I stand, dressed in my satin cowboy suit, ready to sing some pure Americana.

So audiences know from the outset that I'm a Baptist. And at the end of the act, when I speak of Christ and sing what I've come to think of as our witness songs, I believe the Holy Spirit takes over and helps us communicate something our show never before could get across.

"If nothing else, we've got the most *different* show in the world," I told Bob. "Nobody else is doing anything like it."

He and I were talking shop, analyzing the act, actually, pondering the changes in it (and in us) as our lives have changed.

"It's much more emotional these days," Bob observed. "More pointed towards God. Before, we emphasized patriotism, God, and country. It's still that way, but you seem to be turning more boldly towards Christ.

"People are reacting to this."

It's amazing where God will take you, I thought.

But where do we go from here? How much more can the show change? And are we beginning to get too square? Audiences undeniably seem to like what we do—their ovations prove it—but is there a danger that we might seem too fanatical?

A few nights later, I decided to ask some of our musicians how they felt about the evolution of our act. I figured they'd be good critics.

Their reactions surprised me. "To be perfectly honest, I felt sort of negative toward some of those numbers at first," one man confessed. "I thought the music was very square and not with it. I expected this type of song to bomb."

I thought back to our first "bomb"—a spiritual titled "He's Got The Whole World in His Hands." At one time that was our final number, carefully chosen so as to show our audiences what we stand for. Instead of bombing, it brought down the house.

"People's reaction to 'Whole World' was a revelation to me," Bob said. "It seemed to convince the musicians; consequently, their reactions changed. They used to play this music like they were doing us a favor. Now, after every show, someone always mentions that it's a real inspiration to play these dates."

I felt positively astounded. The only way you can survive in the highly competitive pop music field is to keep your fingers firmly on the public pulse. Musicians don't get paid to be idealistic, but to succeed—to know what audiences want and to give it to them.

Several of our musicians told us they really get something extra out of doing our show. "Sometimes guys actually buy their way out of a previous booking in order to do yours," one man told me. "They love doing it. They like this act and what it stands for.

"Somehow it's different. There's something here I just can't explain—a feeling." he shrugged.

I thought back to two sellout concerts we did recently at Fort Myers, Florida. Our conductor had gone ahead of us to rehearse the musicians. As soon as Bob and I arrived he told us, "This is the place where we should include 'How Great Thou Art.' "

"Oh, no!" I gasped.

Impossible! Our full fifty-minute program included several killers: "Power and Glory," "God Bless America," and "Battle Hymn" among them—and I knew I'd sing my insides out by the end of the show. So I was reluctant, even a little annoyed, at his suggestion.

"But I know it's right for these people," he insisted.

And it was. Our musicians have become so attuned to us that they knew "How Great Thou Art" would go, and be a smash. We got a standing ovation on both shows.

One of our most difficult and annoying tasks these days is that of finding suitable pop songs to present in our act, or on television. We like to keep up with what's new and popular, but we're finding more and more songs with lyrics we refuse to offer our audiences.

"Parents would go in and smash half of their kids' rock records if they ever bothered to listen to the words," I told Bob.

"I wish they would," he muttered.

The disgraceful lyrics in many of our current pop songs infuriate Bob. Parents really ought to know how many rock tunes actually promote anti-American themes, or glorify such things as drugs, whiskey or extra-marital love.

Much as we want to keep our act up-to-date, we won't include such numbers. "This show reflects our family and what we stand for. We'll never do anything that's not suitable for any family in America to see," Bob says.

If this results in our act's becoming square, then so be it. And maybe we're getting that kind of reputation, judging from a story one of the fellows told us.

Seems he had a friend in the recording business who said he didn't care much for Anita Bryant.

"Now wait a minute," our guy said. "Have you ever really met her? Do you know Anita?''

The man admitted he didn't know me. He's a person who likes Frank Sinatra, Sammy Davis, Jr., and the real swingers like that, so he figured me as being too much the goody-goody type. But the fellow listened to a couple of my patriotic and sacred albums anyhow and thawed somewhat—but said he still didn't care too much for me.

Later my critic came to one of our performances. He sat through the whole act (he could have walked out after all!). Afterwards he said, ''Gee, it was great! I stood for the ovation right along with everybody else!''

This really meant something to me. Everybody can't like our act, after all. Still this cool cat, who didn't buy the show himself, did acknowledge that it's real. He felt impressed by our simple kind of sincerity—an ingredient that comes up missing in so many forms of entertainment today.

''It's in show business that you need to witness,'' Bob has told me again and again. ''You know that more often than not, this is one of the dirtiest, phoniest businesses there is, Anita.

"If you're sincere about Jesus, tell about Him here. Don't save Him for Sunday school and church, but go out into the world for Him."

Bob and I had strong disagreements about that at first. I didn't believe in displaying my deepest inner convictions to strangers, or in parading my Christian beliefs before secular audiences.

But, like some of our musicians, I've changed a lot!

I've seen the power of God's Holy Spirit at work within me and others as we reach toward our audiences—and they respond.

Where there's a real longing—a true need—God will supply. He'll use me or you or anyone who really wants to be used. Now the guys who play our music see that God can use them too. This really thrills me!

So where does our act go from here?

Who knows? I just hope Bob and I, with our really great guys, will simply try to keep in tune. Not just in tune with one another and with show business, which we all love, but with God's business as well.

12 "We're in This Together"

"Bobby and Gloria, I saw a real nice thing in the airport the other day. Something very sweet," Bob began. Both children gazed at their daddy inquiringly and continued to munch their breakfast toast.

"A man about my age was meeting an older man—maybe about the age of Farfar. The older man must have been a Jew—he had a long white beard, and was dressed all in black. And I suppose the younger man must have been his son.

"Anyhow, when they reached one another, the young man put his arms around the old man—and then he kissed him. Right in front of all those people.

"And that's when I thought of you kids and wished you'd seen that. Because we've been talking about how to show the love we feel—how we shouldn't be ashamed to show love for people."

There was quite a silence around the breakfast table now. Each of the three seemed absorbed in his own thoughts, and for once, neither child offered a comment.

Did they really understand such abstract conversation? If you could have seen the pensive look on Bobby's face, the series of expressions that crossed it then, you'd know he did. As I watched our son, I thought I almost could see the wheels turning in his young mind.

He was imagining himself meeting Bob at the airport, no doubt. Bob would be the age of Farfar, Bobby the age of Bob. Bobby would put his arms around his father—and then he'd kiss him. In front of all those people.

They're so much alike, I thought for the thousandth time. Bob and Bobby—both so sensitive—so affectionate.

Gloria, too, had a faraway look in her eyes. Last night she had confided to me that she had witnessed to Wendy. "I said, 'Wendy, why don't you go to Jesus about that? Jesus can do miracles. He can even heal heart attacks and bad stuff like that. Ask Jesus to help you!'"

Could this be my timid six-year-old? I saw a new maturity—a sureness—in Gloria that caught me by surprise, even as I wondered where she'd heard of "heart attacks and bad stuff like that."

But there's very little time for reflection at our house in the mornings. Soon there was the usual stampede of tooth-brushing, grabbing of books, finding the lost pair of shoes, kisses for Mommy and Daddy, and they're off to school. After they leave, the silence sometimes is deafening!

This day, however, echoes of things our older son and daughter had said lingered in my mind. "Mommy's being a fisherman," Bobby had told his father the night I tried to comfort Mary.

"Jesus can still do miracles," Gloria confidently told Wendy.

Yes, I'm thankful they believe. And now, Lord, You're going to have to make me become as a little child. Because today I'm going to hit some tennis balls with Charlotte Topping. Maybe there'll be an opportunity to say some of the things on my heart. And I'm so scared!

(Possibly this is the place to say that everything that follows comes by the grace of God, and the grace of our friends involved in this story. This is their Christian testimony as well as my own, and they offer it freely—to the glory of God.)

Though Charlotte and I had certain contacts, mostly through our children's school activities and sometimes because of tennis, you wouldn't call us intimate friends. She knew me as a Christian, of course, and I knew she was seeking.

Otherwise, I merely saw Charlotte as a calm, capable gal, very attractive and intelligent, and an excellent mother. And that's about it. How to approach her about the things that lay closest to my heart? I had no idea!

I only knew I must. Bob and I had felt a burden for this couple for so long. Dan's health had troubled him for many months now. Severe emphysema and other complications had sent him to the hospital several times. His physical outlook seemed pessimistic; his emotional one appeared equally bleak.

Dan Topping, very much a man's man, probably feels most at home in the sports world. A few years ago he owned a famous baseball team—the New York Yankees.

At Shea Stadium last summer, the night Dan brought his family to hear Billy Graham preach, even the gatemen greeted him by name.

"Hello, Mr. Topping!" seemed to come from all sides as we moved through the huge stadium.

But the Dan for whom I felt concern was a man now in really precarious health—a rich, sophisticated, successful, worldly man—father of five handsome children under age fourteen, husband of a vital and attractive woman in her thirties. Yet this man who apparently had everything to live for, had, something told me, lost hope.

Why? The answer eluded me.

It's really none of your business, I told myself. How dare you meddle in these lives? Yet I knew this wasn't so. I had a burden, a genuine concern, for Dan Topping. Meddling was not my motive. Still, I felt uncertain and fearful of approaching Charlotte about something so intimate as her family's need for God.

So that day on the tennis courts I had no intention of witnessing to Charlotte, but I knew I must confide to her the burden I felt for Dan. Suddenly the way seemed to open up.

"Charlotte, why don't you come home with me and see the twins?"

Pure inspiration! Charlotte loves the babies. However, I'd pulled a sneaky, because I knew the twins would be napping for at least another thirty minutes to an hour. Sure enough, they were asleep when we got home, so I took Charlotte upstairs on the pretext of seeing some new dresses I'd bought. Meanwhile I prayed not to offend her. *Jesus, help me say the right words,* I pleaded silently. All the time I was thinking about Dan.

Upstairs, I faced my friend abruptly.

"Charlotte, can I level with you? Can I be perfectly honest about something that's been bothering me?"

"Sure," she said, looking at me kind of funny.

"I've been real concerned for Dan," I began. "Not just his physical condition, but I think there's something missing in his life. He's searching . . . . Not that he's said so, but . . . I have the feeling he's lost the will to live—lost hope—and he seems so lonely and lost.''

Charlotte simply looked at me with an odd, unreadable expression on her face. I plunged on. ''I want to tell Dan about Christ,'' I said. ''I feel led to do this, but I don't want to butt into your business.''

There was a dead, heavy silence in the room for a long moment. I wondered what in the world my friend would say—and then she began to talk.

Suddenly the capable, self-possessed woman was spilling everything. And what a tragic, yet typical, story it seemed. Here's a couple who, faced with extremely difficult circumstances, grow apart. He is ill—seriously and chronically—and becoming increasingly more bitter, hopeless, despondent, unwilling to help himself.

''He won't even give up smoking,'' Charlotte said. ''Even though it's killing him.''

Faced with the fear of losing her husband, and with the necessity of caring for five children, Charlotte had to make a hard and necessary choice. Dan was copping out on life, she felt. She'd have to choose between becoming his full-time nursemaid and neglecting their children, or taking proper care of their children and letting her husband and marriage go. What an impossible dilemma!

We talked all afternoon. The scope of this girl's problems, her stark honesty in approaching them, the depth of her pain and despair, pierced my heart. I felt terribly moved by her situation, yet powerless to help. At last I spoke.

"Charlotte, you've become so terribly miserable, bitter, and upset," I said. "You can't keep going this way, or you're going to break."

"I'll never break. I can't! Not until my children are grown," she said. I marveled at her utter conviction.

"And then what, Charlotte? Will your life be over? You'll still be a young woman then."

And I began witnessing to her, pleading with all my heart, because surely it must be Charlotte the Lord meant me to reach. Why else would she open up to me this way?

I say that this woman really cared for her husband, that if Christ would change him, she'd be so glad—but she had no hope.

"Don't you see you must get right with the

Lord?'' I asked her. ''You're going to crack unless you let Him help you. You need God desperately.''

''No. I can't give in,'' she said. By then she'd begun to pace the floor and cry. I'd never before seen Charlotte cry.

''I can't give in,'' she repeated. ''If I give in I'll just crumble.''

How well I understood! I'd been at that very same spot not too many years earlier and—like Charlotte—had realized my own marriage was at stake. I had to tell her.

''It's not a matter of giving in,'' I urged. ''It's a matter of letting God take over. You can't bear these problems alone, Charlotte. Nobody could take what you're taking and stand it for long. You're doing a tremendous job—but it's not enough. Your strength will not be sufficient. You must turn your burdens over to God. Otherwise you'll wreck everything.''

She continued to shake her head, anguished. It wasn't enough. I couldn't find the right words.

Lord, help me! I prayed silently, desperately.

''Look, Charlotte, I've been through this

too. I can testify as to what God will do for you," I said. My words sounded strangely forceful and deliberate. I felt a new surge of energy and determination.

"You deserve the best in life, and you're not getting it. Spiritually you're *dead!*"

Don't ask me where I got the courage. God really laid it to me, so I was able to tell her point-blank she was lost. Probably she'd never realized that.

"Charlotte, can you pray with me?"

"No. Not now," she said dully. "I can't do it. I'll break down—and I just can't break down!"

She wanted to walk out then, but I wouldn't let her. I got downright pushy and insisted she sit down in a chair.

"Okay. You don't pray, but let me pray for you," I commanded her. "Let me commit you to Christ until you become ready to accept Him."

That prayer undoubtedly was the most heartfelt one I ever prayed. Everything seemed to depend upon it. The room seemed almost to pulsate with emotion as I said, "Lord Jesus, let your Holy Spirit stay with Charlotte and surround her. And Lord God, whatever it takes to bring this soul to Christ—do it !''

This really got to Charlotte—and to me. We were in this thing together. Silently we embraced and walked downstairs, each of us totally spent.

Where would God take us next? I had no idea. I couldn't tell if anything had been accomplished or not. Then suddenly I heard myself inviting her to come to church with me on Sunday night, and I heard her accepting.

Thank you, Lord. Give us the time . . . and give me the wisdom . . . and the faith.

But I didn't know if there was time enough, or if someone as inadequate as Anita Bryant could hope to help a woman like Charlotte Topping make even a dent in her complicated life.

And it was five o'clock and I hadn't started supper. Suddenly Bob came in and his arms went around me. He gave me an encouraging little squeeze.

''It's great, Anita!'' he rejoiced as I tried to tell him what had happened. ''We'll pray about it later. Right now, though, why don't I go out and get some hamburgers for supper?''

And he was gone. Suddenly my spirits lifted

and a great peace came over me. How great that Bob understands, that he cares with all his heart!

Thank God we're in this together!

13 New Sister in Christ

I put the car in reverse, backed all the way down our block, then dashed into the house.

"Where's the tape?" I yelled at Bob.

"What tape?"

"The new one, 'Abide With Me.' I need it!"

I grabbed the tape and ran, not pausing to answer Bob's inquiring look. How awful if Charlotte Topping and I were late to Sunday night church! Goodness knew I felt apprehensive enough already; so much so, in fact, I'd developed a tension headache nothing would touch.

So much depends on this evening, Lord, I thought.

Bob did not agree. "Don't expect Charlotte to come to Christ tonight," he told me. "It's going to take several weeks. Charlotte's seeking, but she's far from ready."

But *I* was ready. I'd prayed for Charlotte

and talked to her in every way I knew how, and by now I felt completely frustrated and exhausted. I knew absolutely nothing more I could say to her. There seemed nothing more to do.

Then—abruptly—the Lord sent me back home to get the tape of my new sacred album which Bruce Howe, our friend at Word Records, had just mailed us. We could play the tape in the car as we drove to church, a perfectly natural thing to do, and maybe God would speak to Charlotte through the music.

I suppose He did. Or maybe He used the music to calm *me* down, I don't know. Nevertheless, by the time we got to church, Charlotte and I found ourselves in exactly the right frame of mind to receive the message in Brother Bill Chapman's magnificent preaching.

"Here's a man who's totally sold out to God. God really is using him tonight," I told myself, glancing at Charlotte's intent look.

Love and peace, with a quiet but intensely real current of vitality, seemed to permeate the sanctuary. And Brother Bill was so filled with the Holy Spirit, so on fire for Christ, that tears filled his eyes several times as he spoke of Him.

Then our pastor read Second Corinthians 6:2; just one small verse from the Holy Bible, but one which spoke so powerfully, so authoritatively, that my heart literally pounded in my chest:

For he saith, I have heard thee in a time accepted, and in the day of salvation have I succoured thee: behold, now is the accepted time; behold, now is the day of salvation.

Now is the time—now is the day. Did Charlotte hear God's command? I stole another look at her. She seemed totally absorbed; obviously she was drinking in God's Word.

God has been leading Charlotte all along, I realized suddenly. I have nothing whatever to do with this. He has just used me as a little instrument.

So I bowed my head and turned her over to Him. *Lord, I realize this is Your plan and Your will,* I prayed. *Please help me have the strength and patience and tolerance to be faithful and not to stumble before her.*

Immediately an amazing thing happened. My headache vanished completely. A peace fell over me, my anxiety disappeared, and I knew beyond all doubt that Charlotte was in God's hands. Suddenly I felt alert and expectant.

How would God deal with Charlotte tonight?

As the service progressed, I could tell nothing from her face. She continued to watch intently, absorbed in everything that happened. But I could see no evidence of any overwhelming change in Charlotte—or any disposition toward commitment. Bob must be right. It would take several weeks—perhaps several attempts on my part to woo her back to church—plus some patience and determination.

When we sang the hymn of invitation Charlotte listened thoughtfully, as she had to all parts of the service. Then as the second stanza began she closed her hymn book, placed it in the pew, and slipped out into the aisle. Without a backward glance, Charlotte marched toward that altar like a person on fire!

I couldn't believe what I saw. Watching my friend move toward God's altar, I felt overwhelmed by His love—that love that drew her steadily onward. I must go forward, too, I thought, and be a comfort to her.

As I came up behind Charlotte I began to weep. She, on the other hand, stood there as poised and cool as a cucumber. But the Holy Spirit simply swooped over me and broke me. I got on my knees and prayed for her and with her, my arm around Charlotte Topping, and I couldn't control my emotions. I sobbed like a baby. It was as though I literally was broken. It was the most painful sort of tearing-apart process—something I can't describe—something I'll never forget.

"It was like giving birth," I told Brother Bill later.

"That's exactly what it was, Anita," he replied. "You have to go through that sort of pain sometimes in order to know the ecstasy of giving birth to a child of God."

The scene before that familiar altar seemed like a dream. Charlotte, quietly going on her knees—praying to know Jesus Christ as her Lord and Saviour—the counselor revealing to her the Word with certain Scriptures I'd failed to give her—and Charlotte praying the prayer of confession.

"Jesus, come into my heart."

Can I ever hear those words, without my own heart breaking?

"Take away any sin in my life, and use me in any way you see fit," she said, her voice quiet and distinct, filled with peace. Then she added, "Thank you, Jesus, for bringing Anita into my life."

By this time I'd had it. I'd become a heap of water on the floor. I could be no comfort to anyone. Nevertheless, this was pure joy—something I shall remember forever. I felt filled up and overflowing—crying, and painful, yet joyful beyond all description.

It was like nothing else I've ever known in my life. It was as though I had entered another realm. I'll never again be the same woman, I thought.

On the way home I marveled at Charlotte. You could feel the difference in her. Christ dwelt in her. He showed on her face and in her voice. This was a new and peace-filled woman, gentle and aglow with a remarkable, quiet power. I felt a sense of awe when I looked at her.

We both fell silent for a long while, and when we spoke at last, it was quiet talk about prayer, and reading God's Word. We were sisters.

"You have a personal hot line now, Charlotte. Lean on God," I told her. "He will help you bear these burdens. And you and I together will pray for Dan and the rest of the family. You are cleansed of your sins—and you've a new life ahead of you!"

Never will I forget her joyous smile.

And then I was climbing the stairs to our bedroom, exhausted, trying to contain myself. I wanted to be real cool about it so Bob wouldn't suspect anything. But I couldn't.

The minute I entered our room, I started weeping afresh.

"Charlotte's saved!" I cried out between sobs. In a flash Bob was there, his arms went around me, and he began to comfort me.

"Sweet baby," he said, holding me close until all the tears were spent. And then we began to share. Though Bob had been praying for us that evening, he could hardly believe the news. Now he wanted to know all about it, all Charlotte had said, and he continued to be amazed.

Both of us felt so elated we hardly could go to sleep. How wonderful to lie there, rejoicing, sharing, to have such sweetness between us.

And how it thrilled my heart to be able to come home to a Christian man—one who backed me up all the way. Once again I realized how strong a foundation Bob makes for me, and how much I lean on him. My thoughts as I drifted off to sleep at last were prayers of highest joy and gratitude.

The next day Bob drove to the bookstore to pick up a gift for Charlotte—something to commemorate her big day. We decided she'd need an *Amplified King James Bible,* as well as *Little Visits With God,* the book we use for our children's devotions each morning. We knew she'd want to begin immediately to practice daily worship with her children.

And Bob helped me inscribe a *Scofield Reference Bible* for Charlotte. When it came time to write something, my mind went blank. After a long time I wanted to phone Brother Bill or some other of our Christian friends, except I felt foolish that I couldn't think for myself. At last I turned to Bob.

"What in the world shall I say to Charlotte?"

"Why, 'Happy birthday, Charlotte,' of course," Bob promptly replied.

"You're right!" I exclaimed, laughing. "That's it, of course!"

So I wrote, HAPPY BIRTHDAY, CHARLOTTE. BORN AGAIN FEBRUARY 21, 1971. FROM YOUR SISTER IN CHRIST, WITH LOVE, ANITA.

Later Charlotte dropped by our house and picked up her gifts. She seemed quite touched to read the inscription, but the news concerning her homecoming the night before touched me even more.

"I told Dan and the kids, and they're quite curious about what has happened to me," Charlotte said.

"But it's Dan's reaction that surprised me most. He's so pleased about the whole thing."

She smiled shyly. Obviously Dan's attentiveness really excited her. I felt my heart turn over with joy. But there was more—still more—good news. "I've promised the kids I'll take them to 'Anita's church' next Sunday," she said. "They're real eager to see a Baptist service."

I felt flabbergasted. Never had I expected that. The Topping family regularly attended services in their own church, so I hadn't even suggested they accompany us. I simply hoped Charlotte would continue to come to church with me on Sunday nights for a while.

But if I felt suddenly dazed, I realized my friend looked radiant and composed as I'd never before seen her. The woman for whom I felt such a burden always had seemed uptight and nervously self-contained.

But Charlotte Topping had become a different woman—calm, open, and seeking. Suddenly, watching her, Jesus' words bore in on me, *Seek and ye shall find*.

What more could Charlotte Topping possibly find? I wondered to myself.

After all, she'd just received her own salvation.

14 Healing a Hurt

"Anyhow, Wendy, you're not even a Christian!" Gloria had said.

I felt deeply shocked and hurt to hear my daughter say those words. The girls had gotten into a small squabble, jealousy-inspired, actually, and Gloria simply blurted out the worst thing she could think of to say.

"Gloria, if you want Wendy to be a Christian, you must live out your faith before her," I protested. "Above all, a Christian doesn't try to hurt someone that way!"

Now Dot Morrison, Wendy's mother, had driven over to discuss with me what we might do to improve the situation. The whole thing had been building for several weeks, Dot said. Wendy had come home from school on more than one occasion, crying. I felt as unhappy and dismayed about the problem as Dot did.

"Can't you tell Gloria that Wendy is a Christian?" Dot suggested. "I read the Bible to her every night. And I've taught Wendy to pray. So why can't Gloria believe Wendy is a Christian? Why do the other children say such terrible things to her?''

Children are cruel at times, I thought. Because Wendy comes from a mixed religious background—her mother reared as a Protestant, her father a Jew—they say these things to her. How can we best correct this?

Actually, I understood some of the emotions behind Gloria's harsh-sounding words. I knew, for example, that she'd prayed for more than a year that her best friend might accept Jesus Christ as her Lord and Saviour. Even as Gloria had worried about her own salvation, she'd longed also for her little playmate to know Jesus.

There was real concern there. But, in one semispiteful moment, there had been some normal little-girl jealousy which had resulted in sharp, cruel words.

''Is it right for Gloria and the other children to judge who is and who is not a Christian?'' Dot asked.

''Certainly not,'' I replied. ''The Bible warns us, *Judge not lest ye be judged.* But we must remember, these are children.''

Dot's eyes filled with tears then and she simply looked at me. I wondered what to say. Here was a good mother, a woman who sincerely wanted to rear her daughter as a Christian. Yet in my eyes, she herself perhaps was lost. Had Dot Morrison ever made her own commitment to Christ?

"This has done damage in our home," Dot pointed out quietly. "Jack, my husband, has been liberal about allowing me to teach Christianity to Wendy. I read the Bible aloud each night, and he listens too. This year he even has attended church with us on four occasions.

"All this has not been easy. Anita. It requires give-and-take on all sides. This sort of harassment toward our daughter does very little to advance the cause of Christianity, I feel, in my husband's eyes."

Again I apologized for Gloria, and reminded Dot that these are thoughtless children.

"But I can't teach Gloria something I don't believe." I told her. "You read the Bible. You know therefore that in God's Word it says you must be born again before you can enter the kingdom of heaven."

So I witnessed to Dot quite earnestly, reminding her of God's plan of salvation. "I can't tell Gloria for sure that Wendy's a Christian unless you know there's a definite day and time in her life when she accepted Christ as her Lord and Saviour," I said. "Just reading the Bible to Wendy is not enough. There must be a definite commitment. She must invite Jesus to come into her heart."

There was a silence. "I'm not judging you, nor am I judging Wendy," I told Dot. "Gloria loves Wendy. She is concerned. She has prayed for Wendy for as long as she has known her. But Gloria, in her anger, did use those sharp words to hurt Wendy. That was very wrong of her."

"Would Gloria say that same thing to little Laura Morgan?" Dot asked, a little angry now.

"I don't know. However, I don't know if Laura is saved."

"But Gloria wouldn't, would she?" Dot persisted. "Because Charlie and Marabel Morgan are Christians."

"It's true the Morgan home is Christian, and they're born-again believers. Therefore, Gloria would have the impression that Laura will soon find Christ, if she does not know Him already." I said, carefully. "So there is a difference."

Dot's suggestion, of course, was that Wendy's father's being Jewish had prompted the children's unkind remarks. How sad when those of us who profess Christ seem not to love His own people, I thought. But if I love Jesus, I must care about Jack Morrison just as I do Dot and their daughter Wendy. And I must speak up now for Jesus.

"Dot, if you want your daughter to become a Christian, you must pray the prayer of salvation with her," I said. "Ask her if she wants Christ to come into her life. Say that prayer with her. Make sure she's a Christian."

So I laid it on the line with Dot. Though both of us felt upset and bothered, really she was sweet. Nevertheless, I stuck to my position as a Christian. "I've already reprimanded Gloria and we've prayed about this," I told Dot. "She understands what she did wrong. Now we'll talk and pray some more. And you and I must remember, also, this is a child's fuss."

"Well, can't you tell Gloria that Wendy is a Christian—so she'll take my daughter's side in the future?'' Dot asked.

I simply didn't know what to say. There were no words. I just dropped my head, wondering what might heal some of the hurt. Dot had the strangest look on her face.

"Well, can you at least tell her Wendy's *trying* to be Christian?''

With those words, I suddenly knew this woman was under conviction. God must be using Gloria to reach Wendy and her mother!

"Of course I can say that, Dot,'' I told my friend. "Gloria wants that more than anything.''

Then I told her about Charlotte Topping's conversion of the night before. "Charlotte, who considered herself a Christian, realized she was lost,'' I told Dot. "And only last night she prayed the prayer of salvation and asked Jesus to come into her heart.'' Quickly I shared with her the miracle I'd witnessed the night before.

But as Dot got into her car to drive home, my heart felt heavy. *Lord, what else might I have said?* I asked silently. Somehow I felt as though I had failed.

Later that evening Gloria and I talked some more, then prayed about the hurt Wendy had suffered. Gloria asked Jesus to forgive her for the wrong she had done to the relationship. She also asked Him to help her witness to her little friend by example, not words.

"And now let's leave the whole thing with God," I advised my daughter. "Sometimes after we witness to someone, it's well just to cool it. Let's not even mention all this to Wendy for a while. Let's just see what God can do about the situation."

"Okay, Mommy," Gloria agreed.

So that night at the family altar, we left Wendy and Dot with Jesus.

15   The Summing Up

It's hard to express the ecstasy I feel tonight.

During these few days since Charlotte Topping's conversion, God has brought miracle after miracle to bear. Here I am, for the first time in my life, literally flooded with the power of God's Holy Spirit—*knowing* God's presence in my life—thrilled and awed beyond telling.

Bob and I flew to Indianapolis, Indiana, for a booking on the Friday following Charlotte's conversion. Filled to the brim and overflowing with a new and glorious energy these days I found myself dressed for the trip a full thirty minutes early.

So I joined Farmor and Farfar in the kitchen for a cup of coffee. There the Lord led me to tell Bob's parents about Dan and Charlotte Topping.

To my astonishment, the story brought tears to their eyes. *Dear Lord*, I thought, *You are working in Farmor's and Farfar's lives right now. Help us be sensitive to your plans!*

And then Bob and I were off to Indianapolis, and a meeting I shall long remember. It was a newspaper interview, actually, which took place in our hotel room.

Rita Vandeveer, the bright and pretty young drama reporter from the *Indianapolis Star,* obviously wanted something more than the average, run-of-the-mill feature story. I could tell this young woman likes to dig hard to get something a bit more unusual.

Though this could not help her story, I somehow felt led to share the glorious news about Charlotte and Dan with her. Rita seemed fascinated. Her pencil remained poised above her note pad and I realized, suddenly, that the Lord was leading me to witness to this young writer.

Step by step we engaged, Rita and I, in serious witness. The Lord seemed to show me that she was seeking Him. My heart opened and spilled some of the torrential feelings which had gathered there during the most recent weeks of our lives.

Then I was telling Rita about God's plan of salvation. And we dropped to our knees there in the hotel room and prayed together, until Rita prayed the prayer of confession!

I could only wonder. Nothing like this ever had happened to me before. Earlier, I'd never encountered such clear signs of someone's seeking Christ—not within a stranger, at any rate. And if I *had*, my natural fears, my timidity, would have turned me off.

"Do you think her experience is real, that it will last?" Bob asked as we flew back to Miami Beach.

"I don't know, Bob. That's with God," I told him. "I don't worry about things like that any more. I'm learning how to yield more and more of my nature every day." And, to my great amazement, that's true.

Maybe that's why I felt so peaceful—so joyous and unafraid these past days. Me worry? Ha! The gal who sat down only a few short weeks ago and actually *thought up* a few things to worry about—well, that girl no longer exists.

"Oh, I know I'm a worrywart by nature, but God has shown me a new way to live. I told Charlotte to 'let go and let God,' " I said to Bob. "And you know what? I'm beginning to see that's pretty good advice!"

Back home, we discovered Bobby had come down with chicken pox. Bob promptly acquired a fine case of flu, and joined our son in sick bay. That was Saturday, the day before Charlotte and I planned to attend Northwest Baptist Church with all five of her kids.

Lord, the devil has stepped in and wants to keep me home from church tomorrow, I prayed. You'd better step in and make Bobby's chicken pox and Bob's flu the lightest cases on record, if You plan for me to attend church with the Toppings!

And He did. Accordingly, Charlotte and Gloria and I sat with Robert, thirteen, Tommy, eleven, Johnny, nine, Jimmy, eight and Leigh, the seven-year-old Topping daughter, in one long row. It was a great service!

Then came the hymn of invitation. Gloria tugged at my skirt. "Mommy, I want to go forward."

"Why?"

"I don't know, Mommy, but something tells me I should." Then suddenly I perceived a vision of God's purposes. Perhaps this little girl was meant to witness to the five Topping youngsters!

"Why don't you go ask the church to pray for Wendy to be saved?" I suggested.

"Oh yes, Mommy. That's it!" Gloria's face absolutely glowed as she hurried down the aisle toward the altar.

That started it. The talk, the explanations, among the five young Toppings—their mounting interest in becoming saved—their desire to commit their young lives as they'd seen their mother do.

The following Sunday their three youngest went forward and made their public commitment. Gloria, my timid child, took Leigh by the hand and led her to the Lord! By now there was much conversation between Charlotte and Dan as to whether their seven-, eight- and ten-year-old youngsters knew what they were doing. But after Dan undertook to instruct them, he came to realize they understood their commitment.

"We're united now about our children," Charlotte told me. "Since I came to Christ, Dan and I have had a new closeness I never dared to hope for. A miracle has happened!"

And it had, of course. Not one miracle, but a string of them, all going off like firecrackers in the Topping home—and destined to spread to so many others!

Just eight days following her salvation, the Lord laid it on Charlotte's heart to witness to Dan. I entered into this with her with fear and trembling. Charlotte and I had agreed Brother Bill should be there. Accordingly, on March 1, early in the morning, the three of us approached a rather unwilling Dan.

"If you see I'm achieving any rapport at all with him, start praying," Brother Bill instructed. And that's what I did.

Dan Topping and Brother Bill Chapman seemed to like one another on sight. Typically, Brother Bill wasted no time in turning to the Gospel. Dan, for his part, asked some very penetrating questions, which seemed to please Brother Bill a lot.

"What is hell like?" Dan asked at one point.

Brother Bill immediately read Mark 9:43-48 to us, and I shuddered at the first real vision of hell I'd ever had.

But it was the Good News on which our pastor mainly dwelt. The great promises from Romans 10:9–10 spoke to all of us:

That if thou shalt confess with thy mouth the Lord Jesus, and shalt believe in thine heart

158

that God hath raised him from the dead, thou shalt be saved.

For with the heart man believeth unto righteousness; and with the mouth confession is made unto salvation.

Then Brother Bill added the magnificent verse thirteen: *For whosoever shall call upon the name of the Lord shall be saved.*

Suddenly I glanced at Charlotte. We signaled one another with our eyes, and silently we began to pray for Dan Topping with all our hearts. Brother Bill was reading the third chapter of John now, and as he read the vivid account of Jesus and Nicodemus, Dan looked literally dumbfounded. The truth convicted him. You could see how terribly much Dan longed to be born again.

"You've sold me. I'll be at your church Sunday," Dan said at last. *Praise the Lord!* my heart shouted within me. Then I spoke up for the first time.

"Dan, the Lord may come before next Sunday. If you truly want Him in your life He can come now. Why not take Him right this minute?"

I could not believe my ears. Was this Anita Bryant, speaking out so boldly for Christ?

And then the four of us got on our knees, each of us weeping. Charlotte . . . Dan . . . Brother Bill . . . me . . . none seemed to feel the least embarrasment, only joy. Tears of such intense joy!

Lord God, the wonderful thing is, Charlotte has led Dan all the way, I thought. *And what if I had not listened to You? What if I had failed to speak to Charlotte?*

The following Sunday at our church, Charlotte and Dan came forward together and made a public commitment to Christ. Then Charlotte was baptized. Dan's physical condition demanded that he wait for baptism, however.

"I'm not disappointed," I told Bob. "God has a certain time, a special date, set aside for Dan. I'm learning to realize our God has a perfect timetable for each life."

Maybe that's why I no longer fret about Bob's becoming the spiritual head of our household. God clearly is working in Bob's life, just as He has taken hold of me. A few days ago Fahla, Farmor and Farfar's dog, died. This distressed these gentle people terribly

"Gee, I wish dogs went to heaven," Bob said. "Then I could witness to my dad. I wanted so much to tell him he'd see Fahla again in heaven."

"Oh, Bob, I don't think the Lord would mind if you'd lie just a little bit—about that," I teased him, a bit wistfully.

Just turn this over to God, something inside me said. Don't worry. If you love Farmor and Farfar, how much more perfectly does their Heavenly Father love them.

God continues to pour out His blessings. Leigh, Jimmy, and Johnny Topping, the three youngest of the children, were baptized one evening. Johnny, nine, has begun to witness to everyone in sight—friends, schoolteachers, everyone—with real power.

Charlotte's sister, Bobbie Raye, moved by the new spirit in her sister's home, also came forward in our church and recommitted her life to Christ. Still later Robert, thirteen, the oldest son, was baptized. Tommy, eleven, has not yet taken that step, but we continue to pray for him. The Lord will guide him.

Charlotte will understand when I say, however, that for me the *real* miracle transpired the night her beloved Dan was baptized a Christian. You see, perhaps my Bob had a part in that!

Bob felt led, with Brother Bill, to spend an afternoon praying, witnessing, and reading the Bible with Dan Topping. "I was scared to death, but would have gone alone if Brother Bill couldn't make it," Bob confessed. "It's so difficult for me to witness!

"Anita, I've got to study the Bible. My going to Dan to witness was like sending a minor league pitcher into a major league game. No wonder I was scared."

Despite his fears, Bob acted on his faith. Imagine his joy when, the following Sunday night, he saw his Christian brother baptized. It was on God's timetable!

Dot Morrison phoned me with fantastic news the other night.

"Today Marabel Morgan wound up her class 'Total Woman,'" she told me. "Marabel taught us something she called the 'plan of salvation.'

"Anita, I realized that is what you were talking about the other night—that prayer you kept asking me to pray, and to teach Wendy. Anita, I did pray that prayer. I went home and helped Wendy ask Jesus to come into her heart. That same night, when I went to bed, I asked Him to come into my heart, too.

"Well, things have been different since then. Better somehow, though I can't exactly put my finger on it. And this morning, when Marabel told us about the plan of salvation, it dawned on me why.

"Anita, Wendy and I have been saved!"

Dot Morrison was crying now, and so was I. This news seemed almost too wonderful to bear.

"Call Marabel right away," I begged her. "Oh, Dot, she'll be so thrilled!" Beside myself with joy and thanksgiving, I dashed away to share the good news with my daughter.

How good God is!

This sort of joy, such intense mountaintop experiences, can't last forever. Indeed, such ecstasy would be unbearable if it were prolonged indefinitely on this earth.

The devil doesn't permit that if he can help it, of course. He got busy with me immediately via my hot temper, certain business inconveniences, and some important relationships. There have been some real trials and temptations lately, even among these fantastic victories.

"Still, God has given us such glorious glimpses of what may be ahead," I told Bob. "He has let me witness without fear. He has taken away my pessimism, at least for a while. And, most of all, He has led me into witnessing for Him. He gave me the courage to lead new souls to Christ!"

We fell silent then, wondering at the magnificence of our six short weeks just past.

"If I hadn't obeyed Him about Mary . . ." I began.

"Yes. You had to witness to Mary so you could be free to speak to Bill. And bringing Bill to Christ helped you witness to Charlotte. And witnessing to Charlotte . . ." Bob said, and fell silent.

"It's like ripples on a pool, Anita. Widening and ever widening, so far beyond anything we can even see. But remember, it all began with that first little act of obedience. You listened to God when He led you to Mary."

"But Bob. . . ."

"What?"

"You and the children were praying for me that night. I'm sure I never could have found the courage to witness to Mary without your prayers."

He smiled. "We're all in this thing together, Anita."

Then came the letter from Rita—a long, beautiful, poetic witness that made our hearts sing with excitement. It was a long letter, a really great one, and I'd like to share one significant part:

Another reason why religion has become so important to me is because in a couple of years I want to adopt a little girl, and little girls should have a religious background. I've been thinking about this for ages, and I'm so excited that single people can adopt now. I know it's hard to get a baby, but I don't especially want one anyway. There are so many older kids who need a home more.

Couples are even having trouble getting babies now, but I'm sure I'd be able to get an older child. Even if I do marry, I want to do it anyway. But the point is, when and if this should happen, you can have the satisfaction of knowing that, if your church works out for me, you will have been a "package deal" witness!

Ripples. They continue to widen and widen. How glad I am that Rita Vandeveer happened to be within the circle! And Mary . . . the Toppings . . . the Morrisons . . . Becky . . . oh, how could I even name them all?
. . . oh, how could I even name them all?

"Just a few short weeks ago, looking at our family life, I thought nothing could possibly surpass the blessings we already had." I marveled to Bob. "Now look what God is doing. He's showing us how to live in Christian community."

Imagine! Soon Bob and I, with our two older children, will travel to the Holy Land to see some of the places where Jesus walked. Charlie and Marabel Morgan, who've become real prayer buddies to Bob and me, will go with us.

We knew we'd need a baby-sitter for the kids. Imagine how we felt, therefore, when the Lord provided a really gorgeous one for us—in an amazing way.

Kathie Epstein, a devout Methodist teen-ager, received a trip to the Jerusalem Prophetic Conference as a graduation gift from her father. Bob and I met Kathie in Mobile, Alabama, where I co-hosted with Ed McMahon America's Junior Miss Pageant, and where Kathie represented her state as Maryland's Junior Miss.

Later in a random conversation during pageant rehearsal breaks, Kathie and I discovered we were going to be in the same place at the same time. She agreed to baby-sit for us some during the conference.

So many sweet things happen these days. Like Charlotte Topping's surprise gift to me after she and Dan were saved: a pin shaped like a fishhook. I treasure it!

There was mother's letter telling how Daddy George, my dear stepfather, was baptized the very night Dan Topping was!

And the night Charlie and Marabel Morgan—born-again believers who often came to church with Bob and Me—suddenly decided to become baptized, and become part of our church family.

My heart overflowed that night. So many of those we love crowded into one long pew, to share Charlie and Marabel's moment of decision. I thanked God as I glanced down the long row: the Morrisons, the Topping family, my Bob, and Thomasine.

But Thomasine is somebody particularly special. She's the first soul Charlotte Topping has won to Christ. "I'm your daughter, so she's your granddaughter, Anita," Charlotte informed me gaily.

After church we all had a pizza party at Marcella's *My Kitchen* Restaurant in North Miami, and a birthday cake for Charlie and Marabel. Brother Bill Chapman and Peggy, with Brother Jimmy Johnson, our visiting revival preacher, joined us. Brother Jimmy, it turned out, knew more than any of the rest of us about Jews and Judaism . . . except, of course, for Jack Morrison. We're beginning to feel a hunger to understand Jesus better *as a Jew.* Maybe Jack will help us with that.

How exciting this life can get! Leigh and Johnny Topping, with their mother, went before the church to become fishermen. This means they pledged to witness daily for Christ, to make church visitations, to become "fishers of men" in whatever ways God asks.

As if this weren't enough, that same Sunday

evening Charlie Morgan felt pressed to go to the altar and make the same Christian commitment—led by his good friend, Bob Green! And so it was very fitting, on Bob's birthday, for me to present him with a set of handmade gold cuff links with fish hooks on them. I wrote on the birthday card, "To my darling husband, who is now the head fisherman of the Green family."

And so we grow in Christian experience, in love and outreach, sometimes through trials and temptations, but always in the boundless, amazing grace of God.

There's a verse in the Bible, God's Word, which sums up how I feel tonight. John 21:25, the final verse of the last Gospel, seems to say it all:

And there are also many other things which Jesus did, the which, if they should be written every one, I suppose that even the world itself could not contain the books that should be written. Amen.

Amen and Amen!